The Trust Economy

The Trust Economy

A Second Great Renaissance

AI Is Changing What People Can Do.

When Intelligence Becomes Abundant,

What Happens Next?

Not a world of less humanity,

but a world of greater possibility.

David Drillick

AILEFANT
BOOKS

Published by Ailefant Books

Largo, Florida

ailefantbooks.com

Cover and interior design by the author.

ISBN 979-8-9977323-0-1 — Softcover

ISBN 979-8-9977323-1-8 — Hardcover, Case Laminate

ISBN 979-8-9977323-2-5 — Hardcover, Dust Jacket

ISBN 979-8-9977323-3-2 — eBook, EPUB

Library of Congress Control Number: 2026923095

First Edition, September 2026

Printed in the United States of America

A Note on the Stories

This is a work of nonfiction, but some of its stories are not. Sawtooth Outdoor Adventure Products, Beau-Teak, and the people associated with them are fictional, created to explore the ideas in this book through situations that might occur in the real world. Other people, companies, organizations, and historical events discussed in these pages are real and are identified in context.

Artwork was created using AI, and AI was used to help organize and facilitate the writing of this book.

Foreword

When you explore the writing style of David Drillick in this treasure of stories, you will find it wrapped around one of the most important crossroads of history we humans are facing today in the twenty-first century.

My experiences as a business professional over the decades, in many diverse fields, led me to hunt for and explore the best ways of reaching my customers and clients with the products and services I could provide.

The last job in my career was as a radio station manager. I remember our meetings with the production team each week, making sure our clients' commercials were being placed, while at the same time being approached by program syndicators from across the United States offering their nationally known stars, programs, and news.

I was told at that time that our nation's internet infrastructure was going to become seamless and cost-effective, provide quality sound, and help cut staffing.

That job, and my new understanding of what was happening, led me and my wife into the favorite business of my career. We started a publishing company.

We built a media company called Spectrum Media Group, initially publishing a magazine that grew to 96 full-color pages. It provided expert information and advice from some of the best schools, doctors, hospitals, and healthcare specialists, along with great entertainment partners such as Disney and Universal, throughout the Tampa Bay region and beyond.

At the same time, the technology of the internet was becoming a growing force in media communications. Our team of editors, writers, and designers expanded into a website—then often called a web channel—and email newsletters for our readers and media partners. That expansion grew into broadcasting, including a radio show, as well as weekly events in six locations targeted toward families with children.

As a company, we were top-heavy, as were many print companies. Eventually, like most print publishers, we came to realize that the world was quickly moving into the internet world, with Amazon, Audible, and a zillion others.

I had watched one technological change reshape an industry and a business I loved.

That experience is part of what I brought with me when I read The Trust Economy.

David is able to set the stage seamlessly with a magical story format that is simple and easily understood. You will also absolutely enjoy the classic etched artwork that is timeless. He takes us through where we have been, where we are, and where we could dream of being—as individuals and, yes, as businesses.

I hope you will explore this book as I have. I think you will find yourself enthusiastically enchanted and excited by the simple and fun way David tells the story, while exploring some very important questions about the future ahead of us.

My hope is that he will continue to write more to help us across this crossroads as the world changes into its next cycle.

Jack Hall
Co-Founder, Spectrum Media Group

CONTENTS

APPENDICES

Preface

The Job Advertisement That Started This Book

A small company in Florida was looking for someone to work directly with its president to explore practical uses of artificial intelligence in an ordinary business: research AI tools, learn how different departments operated, identify opportunities for automation and process improvement, test AI in areas such as customer service, marketing, operations, and sales, and help the company figure out what AI could actually do for it.

Assistant to the President — AI Strategy & Business Improvement

One line especially caught my attention:

... *Learn how different departments and company functions operate, then recommend improvements* ...

I applied for the job.

But the advertisement stayed with me. The question kept coming back. How can a business use AI to become better?

I started thinking about it. Every day. I was hooked.

I found that once you start following the consequences forward, the question gets bigger. What happens when the business uses AI? What happens when its competitors use it? What happens when its suppliers use it? What happens when its employees use it?

And then came the question that changed everything: What happens when the customer has AI too?

How This Book Thinks

I am not a futurist, and I'm suspicious of people who claim certainty about what's coming. This book does not try to predict the future. Instead, it follows consequences forward, one step at a time.

It starts with a simple question: where are we, right now? Not where we wish we were, not where the future will supposedly take us — just an honest look at what exists right now.

From there, it asks what a new capability makes possible, separate from any particular product or company. Products come and go. Capabilities tend to stick around and get used, often in ways nobody planned. And once you know what is newly possible, there's a second question, a human one: given what we know about how people behave — what they find convenient, what they respond to — what are they likely to do with it?

Sometimes the reasoning runs the other way. If a particular future looks worth having, you can work backward and ask what would have to be true, be built, and be trusted, for that future to become real.

And underneath all of it is the question that gives the book its shape: if this happens, what happens next? Ask it once, and you learn something. Ask it again about the answer, and then again, and you start to see consequences most people miss — not because they're hidden, but because nobody followed the thread that far.

I don't claim this way of thinking is original. It's closer to how good engineers have always thought about consequences. I just kept applying it to the question that started all of this: what happens to business as artificial intelligence becomes more capable and more widely used?

A Possibility, Not a Prophecy

Nothing in this book is guaranteed. The same capabilities that could distribute trust and expertise more widely could just as easily be used to concentrate power, manipulate people more effectively, or make surveillance more complete than anything before it. I am not going to pretend those futures are not possible, because they very much are.

This book follows one path on purpose — the one where we use these tools to make people more capable, not less; where institutions become more accountable instead of more opaque; where an ordinary person gets something closer to the resources a large organization has always had. When this book describes a future development, read it as a possibility worth examining, and not a forecast.

I don't know whether this is the future we will build.

I want to show you that it's a future we can build.

Why now

You don't have to take any of this on faith about the future. The early pieces are already here.

AI is being used today to compare products, draft documents, summarize feedback, and help people make decisions they used to need a specialist for. What follows explores what may become possible as those capabilities improve, spread, and begin to interact with institutions that adapt around them. Much of what follows requires capabilities already emerging to become better and more widely available, and institutions to begin adapting around them.

That's why it's worth examining these possibilities now, while their shape is still something we can influence, rather than later, once they're simply how things are.

A Second Great Renaissance

The historical Renaissance wasn't the result of a single invention. It emerged from changes in knowledge, art, commerce, technology, institutions, and the circulation of ideas that reinforced one another. It emerged from a thousand smaller changes that turned out to compound.

I don't think artificial intelligence guarantees anything like that. Technology never has. It only creates possibilities. We are the ones who decide what to do with those possibilities. But if even some of what follows in these pages turns out to be true: if expertise really does become more portable, if evidence really does become easier to find, if ordinary people really do end up with capabilities once reserved for large institutions, then we may be looking at something far more significant than a faster or cheaper version of what we already have.

We may be looking at the beginning of a civilizational rebirth.

Not a perfect one. People will still be people, sometimes generous, sometimes not; sometimes careless, occasionally brilliant. This book isn't about fixing human nature. It's about building better systems for the humans we are.

If we manage that, even partly, I think it deserves the name this book gives it.

A Second Great Renaissance.

It is not inevitable.

But it is possible.

Many of the habits and institutions we rely on developed for good reasons. Information was expensive, expertise was scarce, verification took time, and no one person could know very much on their own.

Artificial intelligence is starting to change some of those conditions. When conditions change, the assumptions built on top of them are worth looking at again.

So for the next several chapters, we're going to revisit some familiar territory: trust, evidence, expertise, reputation, verification, capability. Not because the old answers were wrong, but because they were answers to conditions that may be changing.

Let's put the pieces back on the table and look at them again.

Part I

Rethinking the Ground Beneath Us

Chapter 1
The Next Great Transition

History rarely announces that it is changing.

No trumpet sounds. No banner appears across the sky. Most people wake, make coffee, go to work, raise their kids, pay their bills, and reasonably assume that tomorrow will look roughly like yesterday.

That assumption is usually correct. Most days are not historic.

And yet every so often, quietly and without anyone's permission, civilization begins to reorganize itself around something new. At first, the change looks small. A different way to grow food. A better loom. Movable type. Steam. Electricity. A computer. The internet. Each one arrives looking like just another invention — a slightly better version of something we already had. It's only in hindsight that we can see it was something else: not a better tool, but a new capability. And a new capability, once it exists, sends ripples across the whole surface of civilization. Ripples that are, almost without exception, invisible to the people living through the first few of them. It usually takes years, sometimes centuries, before anyone looks back and says: ah, that's when it started.

I think we may be near the beginning of one of those moments now. But before I ask you to consider whether artificial intelligence is one of these transitions, I want to spend a little time on the transitions we already recognize because they tell us something important about how this works, and what to watch for.

The Lost Beginning

We don't know who invented agriculture.

We know it happened. We know it changed nearly everything about how human beings lived. But the people who first noticed that a seed, planted deliberately, would grow into something you could eat again next season — their names are gone. Civilization hadn't yet learned how to remember itself.

What agriculture created wasn't just food. It created the possibility of producing and storing food in one place, which made permanent settlement possible. As settlements grew into villages and towns, trade and administration became more complex. Memory alone was no longer enough. Records became increasingly valuable, and eventually writing gave civilization a way to preserve what a single human memory could never hold on its own.

That was the first great ripple. Notice the shape of it: one capability didn't just solve one problem. It created a cascade of new problems, each of which had to be solved by something that hadn't existed before.

Civilization Learns to Remember

Every generation is born into a world it didn't build.

Language, agriculture, roads, laws, mathematics, medicine: none of us invented these. We inherited them, used them, improved a few things at the margins, and passed the whole collection forward, usually without much ceremony. That quiet handoff, repeated across thousands of generations, is most of what we call "civilization".

It doesn't only happen in books, either. Old roads still tell you where people needed to go. Temples tell you what people believed mattered enough to build something permanent for. Coins tell you how an economy worked, not just how someone wrote that it worked. Every civilization leaves messages for whoever comes after it — some in words, some in stone, some in the shape of a city.

One of the great tragedies when a civilization collapses is how much of what that civilization knew disappears along with it.

Power Beyond Human Muscle

For most of human history, work meant muscle — yours, or an animal's.

Grain was ground by hand, and then by animals turning heavy stones, and then by water, which turned out to be stronger and far more patient than either. Factories gathered next to rivers for the same reason the earliest cities gathered next to farmland: that's where the necessary resource was.

Then steam arrived, and steam is, in a real sense, a portable river. A factory no longer needed to sit beside moving water. It could make its own power anywhere, and railroads could carry that power wherever it needed to go. Industry spread. Cities swelled to match it.

And with that growth came an entirely new list of problems nobody had needed to solve at the previous scale: clean water, sanitation, fire protection, policing, building codes, public transit, urban planning.

The steam engine didn't just make better machines. It forced civilization to invent institutions that had never needed to exist before.

The pattern is worth noticing. The technology is rarely the hard part. The hard part is what civilization has to build around it.

The Age of Information

Language quietly keeps a record of these transitions, if you know where to look. A *secretary* once literally kept secrets. A *clerk* originally belonged to the clergy, back when literacy itself was a specialized skill. A *computer* was, for a couple of centuries, a job title; a person, often a woman, hired to perform calculations for engineers or accountants. Eventually the counting machines took the name because they had already taken the job.

Those machines didn't stay still. Mainframes gave way to personal computers. Researchers linked computers together, and the links became the internet. Email became one of the first things people used it for. The web connected information, search engines organized it, and smartphones put the whole arrangement into billions of pockets. Even our words kept adapting — *programs* became *applications*, and applications became, with the particular disregard young technologies have for dignity: *apps*.

Civilization was reorganizing itself again. Most of us barely noticed because we were too busy living inside it.

The Pattern

Step back far enough and a pattern appears.

Agriculture created abundant food. Printing created abundant knowledge. Industry created abundant mechanical power. Computers created abundant information. Each time, a new capability didn't just improve on the last one — it enlarged what was possible, and then civilization spent decades, sometimes centuries, catching up to it.

That catching-up is the real story, more than the invention itself. Technology moves fast. Institutions move slowly. Most of history is the record of civilization trying, imperfectly, to close that gap.

Our Present Moment

This is where artificial intelligence comes in — later than you might expect, and on purpose.

Most books about AI start with AI. This one doesn't, because I don't think that's where the story starts. Artificial intelligence didn't arrive from nowhere. It's the product of an extraordinarily long chain of things that had to happen first. Without agriculture, there are no cities. Without cities, there's no writing. Without writing, there are no universities. Without universities, there's no modern science. Without science, there are no computers. And without computers, there is no artificial intelligence.

AI isn't separate from civilization. It's one of civilization's newest creations. Which changes the question worth asking about it. The interesting question isn't simply what will artificial intelligence do? It's what kind of civilization is going to decide what artificial intelligence becomes?

Because that's what civilization has always been for: a way of preserving capability, knowledge, and trust across generations that will never meet each other. Every generation inherits what came before, adds something of its own, and decides, deliberately or not, what gets passed on to the next generation. Artificial intelligence is simply the latest thing we've been handed to make that decision about.

It's a remarkable capability. Like every capability before it, it will send ripples outward, and some of those ripples will open up extraordinary opportunities, and others may open up real dangers, and which of those turns out to be true will depend far less on the technology than on us.

Capabilities create possibilities. People create civilization. Institutions help determine which possibilities endure.

This book is not a prediction about artificial intelligence. It's an architectural proposal about what we might deliberately choose to build with it. A framework, not a forecast. It asks one question, stated plainly: If artificial intelligence becomes one of civilization's defining capabilities, what institutions should we build to make sure it strengthens human freedom, dignity, prosperity, and trust, rather than quietly eroding them?

The pages ahead are one possible answer to that question.

I call it *The Trust Economy*.

If civilization keeps getting reorganized by new capabilities, one after another, there's an obvious next question: what makes this particular capability different from all the others that came before it?

Chapter 2

The Age of Intelligence

Every age gets defined by what it learned to multiply.

The wheel multiplied movement. The plow multiplied a farmer's reach across a field. The steam engine multiplied muscle on a scale no ox ever managed. Electricity multiplied what a factory could do after dark. Computers multiplied arithmetic. The internet multiplied how fast an idea could travel from one head to another. Each of these mattered because each one took something humans could already do, and did a lot more of it, a lot faster, for a lot less effort.

Artificial intelligence is a strange animal by comparison, because it doesn't really multiply just one thing.

It analyzes information. Recognizes patterns. Summarizes what would otherwise take you an afternoon to read. Drafts a document. Translates a sentence. Helps you think through a decision you're not sure how to make. None of these, on their own, would be especially remarkable. We've had tools that did versions of each. What is unusual is that one technology is doing all of them at once, and doing them in something like the domain we've always considered most distinctly ours: *thinking*.

That difference is worth taking seriously, and it's why this chapter exists before we go any further.

Humanity Has Always Extended Itself

There's one habit that separates us from every other species we know of: we build things that extend what we can do.

The telescope extended sight far enough to see moons around other planets. The microscope extended it in the opposite direction, down into a world too small to see unaided. Books extended memory across centuries; you can read what a person thought five hundred years ago, which is a genuinely strange power when you stop to consider it. Ships extended how far a person could go. Telephones extended how far a voice could carry. Computers extended how fast you could calculate.

Civilization, looked at from a certain angle, is just the long accumulated record of us extending ourselves, one tool at a time. Artificial intelligence belongs squarely in that history. What sets it apart from the tools before it is where it reaches: not just our hands, or our legs, or our voice, but increasingly the thinking that sits behind all three.

What Each Revolution Removed

Every one of the earlier revolutions loosened a specific limitation. Agriculture greatly increased the amount of food people could deliberately produce from the land. Steam freed man from the limitations of muscle and river power. Electricity removed the limit on when work could happen. Computers quickened the speed at which calculations could be made. And the internet allowed information to reach everyone almost instantaneously.

Artificial intelligence begins to loosen a different constraint — the limits of what one person can analyze, compare, remember, create, and consider unaided. Not entirely, and not perfectly. A single person still only has one head. But AI is already changing how people approach nearly every task that requires thinking, on a scale we haven't seen a technology manage before.

Every previous age multiplied what people could do. This one is starting to multiply what people can think about doing — which is a more unsettling kind of multiplication, because it reaches closer to the part of ourselves we tend to consider off-limits to machines.

Intelligence Starts Behaving Like a Resource

For almost all of human history, intelligence has been bottlenecked by the individual carrying it around.

A brilliant engineer could design one bridge at a time. A gifted physician could see one patient in front of them. An exceptional teacher could only be in one classroom. Knowledge spread exactly as fast as people could explain it to each other, which — measured against the pace of everything else in modern life — is slow.

Artificial intelligence starts to change that arithmetic. One person, working with the right assistance, can often do work that used to require a small team: exploring more ideas, comparing more alternatives, summarizing more research, drafting more documents, catching more patterns — not because that one person got smarter, but because the bottleneck around them loosened. That limiting resource is starting to shift. Not with perfect intelligence, and not with wisdom, which is a different thing entirely, and one we'll come back to. But with capable assistance, broadly available, that lets an ordinary person think farther and across more ground than they could have managed alone.

What AI Is Not

Before this starts sounding like a sales pitch, let me say plainly what artificial intelligence is not.

It has no childhood. No personal memories built from a life lived. No lived experience, no ambitions of its own, no emotions in the sense a human has them, and no demonstrated consciousness.

Whatever else it is, it remains a human creation. It is an extraordinarily capable tool, even if it doesn't always feel like one when it finishes your sentence better than you would have.

Keeping that plainly in view protects against two mistakes that tend to sit at opposite ends of the same misunderstanding. One is treating AI as a novelty; a clever party trick that doesn't deserve serious attention. The other is treating it as something close to omniscient. Neither is true. Getting the future right requires we remember that.

Intelligence Is Bigger Than Logic

People tend to picture "intelligence" as something like chess — solving equations, calculating odds, spotting a pattern in a column of numbers. Those are real forms of intelligence. But human intelligence has never stopped there.

We tell stories. We build metaphors out of nothing and expect other people to instantly understand them. We get jokes, and we get why a joke isn't funny when you have to explain it. We hear sarcasm and know, somehow, that the words mean roughly the opposite of what they say. We invent new words when the old ones won't do. We communicate through music and art and half-finished sentences that our friends somehow complete correctly.

Words carry information, but tone carries emotion, and context carries intention, and shared history carries meaning that would be invisible to anyone standing outside it. Artificial intelligence increasingly participates in a surprising amount of this. It can catch a metaphor, explain a pun, and help translate not just words but the feelings behind them. That doesn't mean it experiences language the way a person does. It means intelligence itself has always been a bigger, stranger thing than pure calculation, and a system that's going to be genuinely useful to people has to understand how people talk to each other, not just what the dictionary says the words mean.

What Stays Different

Still, there's a line worth drawing here, one the book will keep returning to. Artificial intelligence can recognize patterns in how people describe their experiences. It cannot have those experiences. A parent understands what it is to raise a child because they have done it, at three in the morning, more than once. An experienced doctor may understand how to sit with someone in a hard conversation because they have sat in that chair many times before. A soldier understands uncertainty because he's lived it. Life shapes judgment in a way that pattern recognition, however sophisticated, can not replicate.

AI can assist those conversations. It can not replace what produced the judgment in the first place.

Which is why the more accurate way to think about what is coming is not as a contest between people and machines. Rather it is a partnership, where each side brings something genuinely different to the table, and the partnership only works if we're honest about which side brings what.

Every Profession, Differently

Because intelligence touches nearly every kind of work, artificial intelligence too is likely to reach into nearly every profession; from medicine, law, government, and engineering, all the way through to education, finance, journalism, and construction, and even parenting in its own way. Some tasks will end up heavily automated. Others will stay deeply, stubbornly human. Most will land somewhere in between, as an actual partnership of sorts between a person and a system.

The question is no longer if artificial intelligence will show up in these professions. It already has. The live question, the one every profession may have to answer for itself, and probably answer more than once, is simpler and harder: *how should people and intelligent systems work together?*

Capability, Then Responsibility

Technology creates capability. It does not, by itself, create purpose. Artificial intelligence can strengthen freedom, or it can concentrate power in fewer hands than ever. It can widen opportunity, or deepen the gap between who has it and who doesn't. It can sharpen a decision, or accelerate a bad one at a speed no one has time to catch. The technology doesn't decide which of those happens.

People do. Which means the challenge in front of us isn't only technological, it's organizational, ethical, economic, and ultimately civilizational. Artificial intelligence opens up possibilities. Deciding which of those possibilities becomes real is still, entirely, our job.

The Map Isn't Finished

One more thing, before we move on — and I think it's the most honest thing in this chapter.

We are building remarkably capable artificial intelligence while still, in a fairly basic sense, figuring out our own minds. Neuroscience has taught us a great deal about the brain. Psychology has deepened what we understand about memory and learning and behavior. And yet enormous stretches of human thought still happen somewhere below conscious awareness. Where does a sudden insight come from? Why does a problem sometimes solve itself overnight, after you stop consciously working on it? How does intuition catch a pattern before you can explain why you noticed it?

The map of the human mind still has real *terra incognita* on it. The old cartographer's shorthand for the places yet uncharted. We are, in other words, learning to build intelligent machines at the same time we're still discovering what that intelligence in us is. That should produce a certain amount of humility, and I'd like to hold onto that humility for the rest of this book.

Looking Ahead

If intelligence is becoming abundant, there's an obvious next question, and it's not a comfortable one:

does abundant intelligence automatically produce wisdom?

History says no. Information became abundant decades ago. Knowledge became more accessible than at any point in human history. And yet understanding remains hard to come by, and wisdom remains, if anything, rarer than ever. Artificial intelligence doesn't erase that gap. If anything, it makes the distinction between having information and knowing what to do with it more important than it has ever been.

Chapter 3
From Information to Understanding

Here's a question worth asking: if information and intelligence keep becoming more abundant, what becomes scarce?

It's not an idle question. For most of human history, the honest answer to "what's hardest to get" was information itself. Knowledge traveled at the speed of a person walking, riding, or eventually sailing. Books were rare and expensive enough that owning more than a handful of them signaled real wealth. Formal education reached a small slice of the population. An idea discovered in one place might take a generation, or several, to reach somewhere else.

Writing was the first real answer to that problem — a way to preserve knowledge outside a single skull, so it could outlast the person who had it. Libraries collected what writing preserved. Universities organized what libraries collected. The printing press then blew the doors off the whole system, and newspapers, radio, television, computers, and the internet each took their turn accelerating how fast information could be created, stored, and passed along.

Artificial intelligence is the newest link in that chain, and in some ways the strangest one, because it doesn't just help you find information. It can organize it, summarize it, compare it, explain it, and generate new material in response to a question or request.

And here's the paradox nobody quite expected: people have never had more information available to them, and people have rarely felt less certain.

The Noise Problem

Open any search result on a contested topic and you'll find contradictory claims sitting side by side, each stated with total confidence. Experts disagree, sometimes publicly and sometimes about things you'd assume were settled. Studies that appear to measure the same thing produce different answers.

Advertising, opinion, propaganda, and now a rising tide of AI-generated content all compete for the same handful of minutes you have to spend evaluating any of it. There is, simply, more of it than any one person can sort through.

The economic principle is: abundance tends to commoditize; scarcity creates value. When something becomes plentiful enough that everyone has access to it, having it stops being the advantage. For much of history, access to information itself was scarce. Today, enormous amounts of information are readily available. The scarcity has begun to move elsewhere. Which means the defining challenge of this century is knowing which information deserves your trust.

That's a different problem, and it doesn't get solved by making more information available. If anything, more information without better ways to evaluate it just makes the noise louder.

Why Information Alone Isn't Enough

Consider what a piece of information can and can't do on its own. Information answers a question: what, when, how much. It doesn't, by itself, explain how that fact relates to everything else you know, or whether it should change what you do next. That relating and that deciding are different mental operations, and they don't happen automatically just because you've accumulated more facts.

There's a useful way to think about the stages between having a fact and knowing what to do with it. Start with data — raw, uninterpreted: a number, a reading, a transaction. Organize the data and give it context, and it becomes information. Accumulate information over time, connected and retained, and it becomes knowledge. Grasp how pieces of knowledge relate to one another — cause, effect, tradeoff, exception — and you've reached understanding. Apply that understanding to an actual decision, in a specific situation, with real consequences, and you've exercised judgment. Act consistently on sound judgment, in a way others can observe and rely on, and that becomes trustworthy action. Wisdom grows when understanding and judgment are tested by experience over time; when someone learns not only what is true, but what matters, what consequences are likely to follow, and when a principle should or should not be applied.

Wisdom, in other words, isn't just knowing a lot. It's truth so thoroughly understood, through knowledge and experience and judgment and repeated action, that it stops being something a person has and starts being something a person is.

Artificial intelligence can genuinely help at almost every early stage of that climb. It can organize information faster than any person could. It can compare evidence across more sources than you'd have time to read. It can reveal patterns and relationships that would otherwise stay buried. What it cannot do is live your life for you — and it's the living, the accumulated weight of having acted in the world and dealt with the consequences, that turns understanding into judgment and judgment into something like character, and ultimately to wisdom. That last stretch of the climb still belongs to us.

Where the Value Moves

The Information Economy often rewarded access—who possessed information, who could distribute it, and who could find it. As general information becomes abundant and inexpensive, access alone becomes less distinctive. Value moves toward something harder: determining what is reliable, understanding what it means, and knowing what to do with it.

It is no longer enough simply to accumulate facts. Understanding gains value when it can be checked, when it holds up, and when it can be preserved, improved, and responsibly handed to the next person who needs it. That is the same instinct that first drove someone to write things down instead of trusting memory alone—now operating at a much larger scale.

The Question Beneath the Question

As information becomes abundant, the harder question is no longer simply what can I know? It is what can I rely on?

That question matters whenever people must act on knowledge they cannot independently verify. How are strangers supposed to cooperate in a world drowning in information but starving for confidence?

Civilization has had an answer to that question for a very long time, long before anyone had heard of artificial intelligence.

Trust.

It is trust that lets a stranger hand you money for a product they've never tested, hire a contractor they've never worked with, or take a doctor's advice without independently evaluating all the evidence behind it. Trust has always been how we cooperate across the gaps that information alone can't close.

But trust has a problem. It is often difficult to know who or what deserves it.

Artificial intelligence may begin to change the economics of finding out.

The next chapter asks why, in a world where intelligence itself is becoming abundant, trust may be about to become the most valuable resource civilization has.

Chapter 4

The Coming Trust Revolution

Think about what has to go right just for you to drive to work.

You trust that the stranger in the oncoming lane will stay on their side of the double yellow line. You trust that the bridge was engineered by someone who knew what they were doing, and inspected by someone who checked their work. You trust that the mechanic who serviced your brakes last month did what the invoice says he did. You trust that if something goes wrong, an ambulance will show up, and the people in it will know what they're doing too.

None of that trust is dramatic. Most days you don't think about it at all. And that's exactly the point. Trust works best when it's invisible, which is also why it's easy to underestimate how much of civilization runs on it.

Civilization Is a Trust Network

Families depend on it. Communities depend on it. Businesses, governments, markets, schools, science — all of it rests on trust, whether or not anyone involved ever uses that word out loud. Seen from this angle, civilization isn't really best described as a collection of people and buildings and laws. It's more accurate to call it a vast, constantly renewing network of trusted relationships.

Which means it's worth asking what happens when the network frays.

What Distrust Costs

Without trust, cooperation gets expensive fast. People start spending their time verifying claims instead of acting on them, writing contracts to cover every contingency, inspecting work that should have been reliable in the first place, buying insurance against the possibility that someone won't do what they said, hiring auditors, lawyering up, protecting themselves against deception that hasn't even happened yet. Safeguards have real value. Contracts clarify obligations. Inspections catch failures.

Audits can reveal problems. Insurance spreads risk. But the more uncertainty and distrust a system contains, the more resources must be devoted to protection instead of production.

There's a blunt way to say this: one dishonest person can consume the productive effort of hundreds of honest ones, just by making everyone around them a little more careful, a little slower, a little less willing to take a reasonable risk.

Trust runs the equation the other way. When people trust each other, they cooperate faster, decide faster, need fewer safeguards, and spend their energy building things instead of defending against being cheated. Trust multiplies cooperation. Cooperation is one of the foundations of prosperity.

How Trust Learned to Travel

For most of history, trust stayed close to home, because it had to. You traded with your neighbors because you knew them, and knowing someone personally was, for a very long time, the only reliable trust mechanism available. That works fine for a village. It doesn't scale to a civilization.

So civilization built extensions for it. Merchant reputation let a trader's name travel farther than the trader could. Guilds let a stranger trust a tradesman's competence because the guild had already vetted it. Banks developed systems for storing, transferring, lending, and accounting for money across relationships in which the participants often did not know one another personally. Double-entry accounting made it possible to trust a set of numbers without personally watching every transaction happen. Courts gave broken promises somewhere to go. Professional licensing gave strangers evidence that a doctor, electrician, or other practitioner had met an established standard. Consumer brands let you trust a product on a shelf a thousand miles from where it was made. Credit systems let a bank trust a borrower it had never spoken to.

None of these were really separate inventions solving separate problems. They were the same problem, solved again and again at increasing scale: how to extend trust past the limit of personal acquaintance? Every time civilization found a new answer, it could support cooperation among more strangers than before — and every expansion of trust turned out to be, quietly, an expansion of what the whole civilization could do.

Where Artificial Intelligence Fits

Artificial intelligence is the next entry on that list, and it's a strange one, because it doesn't extend trust the way a bank or a guild did. It changes what the question even is.

For most of the history we just walked through, the operative question was some version of *can I find information, can I find this person, can I verify this claim*. As AI increasingly helps people make decisions, evaluate products, negotiate agreements, and manage the ordinary business of daily life, that question quietly shifts. The question begins to shift from: *can AI give me an answer?* to something more important. What that answer based on, and does it deserve my confidence?

An AI system can generate a plausible, confident, well-written answer to almost anything, correct or not. The volume of available answers is no longer the bottleneck. What is scarce is knowing which of those answers, and which people, institutions, and pieces of evidence behind them, deserve your confidence.

As intelligence becomes more abundant, the ability to determine what deserves our trust becomes increasingly valuable.

Trust as Infrastructure

I want to push this a step further than "trust matters", because I think it undersells what is happening. Trust isn't just a nice quality that makes life pleasant. It is infrastructure. In the same category as roads, electricity, and the financial system. Something that mostly stays invisible right up until it's missing, at which point everything built on top of it stops working at once.

Every visible institution in a functioning society is quietly resting on it. A currency only works because enough people trust it will still buy something tomorrow. A stock market only works because enough people trust the numbers it reports are real. Patients enter hospitals trusting that the people treating them have been properly trained, that the medicines are what their labels say they are, that the equipment has been maintained, and that the institution has systems for catching dangerous mistakes.

Pull enough trust out from under any of these systems and the structure begins to collapse. It may not happen all at once. Friction increases. Cooperation becomes harder. Institutions become less effective. But eventually, what was built on that foundation can no longer support its own weight.

Societies that get better at verifying, preserving, and extending trust end up with lower friction, easier cooperation, sturdier institutions, and more prosperity than societies that don't. That's not a moral claim, though it happens to align with one. It's closer to an engineering observation about which systems can function effectively at scale.

The Trust Revolution

Civilization has spent thousands of years working on one problem: making intelligence easier to get. Writing, libraries, universities, the printing press, the internet, and now artificial intelligence are all chapters in that same long project.

That project isn't finished, and probably never will be. But something has changed. For a growing share of humanity, access to information and analytical capability is becoming dramatically easier and less expensive. As that happens, another bottleneck becomes more visible.

It isn't enough to have intelligence available. We need to know which intelligence deserves our trust. After centuries spent making intelligence easier to obtain, we are beginning to confront a different problem: determining what deserves our trust. That is the beginning of the Trust Revolution.

If trust is essential to cooperation, the next question is practical: how do we know what deserves it?

For most of history, finding out has been expensive—testing costs money, investigation takes time, expertise is scarce. Trust may be valuable, but verification has a cost.

What happens when artificial intelligence begins to lower it?

Chapter 5
The Limits of Information

Humanity pulled off something remarkable, and it's worth pausing to give it credit before we talk about its limits.

For most of history, knowledge was scarce in a way that's hard to fully picture now. Books were expensive enough to be treated like family heirlooms. Libraries were rare, and often restricted to people with the right credentials or the right birth. Getting reliable information about almost anything could mean years of study, or travel, or access to an institution that simply wasn't available to most people.

The Information Economy tore down many of those barriers. Search engines put the accumulated knowledge of humanity within reach of anyone with a connection. Smartphones made it portable enough to carry in a pocket. Digital libraries, online education, instant global communication, electronic commerce — an enormous share of modern life exists because information could suddenly be created, copied, and delivered at almost no cost.

This ranks among the genuine achievements of human civilization. Information became abundant on a scale nobody alive a century ago would have believed.

And like every great success, it eventually revealed the limit it hadn't solved.

From Finding to Trusting

The defining challenge of the Information Age was finding information. The defining challenge of the age we are entering is deciding which information deserves your confidence.

By solving the first one so thoroughly, the Information Economy quietly handed the second one to every individual person, without much fanfare. Millions of people now spend real hours every day doing work that earlier generations would barely have recognized: investigating, comparing, cross-checking, trying to figure out who's telling the truth.

The Dishwasher Problem

Consider something as mundane as replacing a broken dishwasher.

Within minutes, a family can pull up hundreds of models. Every manufacturer claims superior performance. Thousands of customer reviews appear, and some of those reviews are genuine, and some are subtly biased, and some were written by an enthusiastic new owner after four days of use who hasn't yet discovered the flaw that shows up in month eight. A few might be outright fabricated.

Professional reviewers disagree with each other. Advertisements highlight exactly the specifications that flatter the product and go quiet on the ones that don't. Repair costs — arguably the single most useful number for a purchase like this — are almost never printed anywhere.

So the family reads reviews, compares spec sheets, watches a few videos, checks a forum thread, texts a friend who bought one last year. Eventually, they buy something. Not because they reached certainty. But because they got tired of investigating, and that fatigue is doing more of the deciding than anyone would like to admit.

Now raise the stakes. Hiring a contractor. Choosing where to put a decade of retirement savings. Same pattern, heavier consequences, and a verification burden that grows in exact proportion to how much is riding on getting it right. The Information Economy didn't just democratize knowledge. It quietly democratized due diligence, and handed everyone a job most people never signed up for.

Verification Is Labor, Not Information

Information is a fact. Verification is the work of deciding whether that fact deserves your confidence. Comparing evidence, recognizing genuine expertise, spotting bias, noticing a conflict of interest, catching what's conspicuously missing, checking whether independent sources agree, and exercising judgment on the occasions when they don't.

That's labor. It takes time, experience, knowledge, and sustained attention, which is precisely why verification has always been expensive, even in an age when information itself became almost free.

Digital information can be copied and distributed at extremely low marginal cost. Verification, historically, has remained much more labor-intensive.

What Civilization Already Built for This

None of this is a new problem, even if AI is a new answer to it. Reducing uncertainty before acting is one of the oldest human instincts there is, and as societies grew into civilizations, that instinct got built into institutions.

Merchants standardized weights and measures so a pound in one town meant the same thing in the next. Guilds certified that a craftsman's skill met an established standard. Governments built courts to enforce promises that got broken. Universities certified that a student had completed an established course of study. Professional bodies set qualifications for who could practice medicine or law. Independent laboratories tested whether a product did what it claimed. Independent accountants examined financial records against established accounting standards. Organizations like Consumer Reports and Underwriters Laboratories built entire institutions around the single job of testing things independently, on the public's behalf rather than the manufacturer's. Building inspectors verified that construction met code before anyone moved in.

Different industries, different centuries, same underlying function every time: reducing uncertainty for someone who couldn't reasonably verify it themselves. Verification creates value precisely because it removes uncertainty that would otherwise be expensive, or dangerous, or both, to carry.

When the Cost of Verification Changes

Civilization built verification institutions because verification was expensive. AI may change that cost

For decades, digital technology made information dramatically cheaper to find and distribute. AI has the potential to go a step further: properly designed, it can help make verification itself dramatically less expensive.

A search engine helps answer, *Where can I find information about this?* AI, used well, can increasingly help answer a different question: *Which of this information deserves confidence, and why?*

Finding retrieves. Verification evaluates.

Information learned to scale. Verification, historically, did not. That may be about to change.

When Verification Gets Cheap

Picture asking an AI assistant something like: find the most reliable dishwasher under nine hundred dollars — one that cleans well, has low repair costs, and has held up over time.

A sufficiently capable assistant could do more than search. It could investigate. It could weigh independent sources against each other, notice where thousands of reviews agree and where a handful of outliers stand out, catch contradictions between what's claimed and what's demonstrated, and tell you plainly when the available evidence just isn't good enough to answer confidently. The willingness to say I'm not sure is a large part of what makes an assistant like this trustworthy rather than merely fast.

As verification gets cheaper, better decisions get easier across the board. Consumers choose more wisely. Businesses spend less time vetting suppliers. Employers may be able to evaluate candidates more accurately. Investors act with more genuine confidence instead of borrowed confidence. And markets, gradually, start rewarding demonstrated reliability over merely persuasive advertising, because reliability becomes something an ordinary buyer can increasingly check before making a decision.

A New Economic Arithmetic

Economic transitions often occur when something previously scarce becomes substantially more abundant or less expensive.

This next transition may be different. Artificial intelligence creates the possibility that verification itself could become dramatically less expensive and more widely available.

And that changes the arithmetic all the way down. When verification gets cheaper, trust gets easier to establish. When trust gets easier to establish, cooperation gets cheaper. And when cooperation gets cheaper, entirely new kinds of commerce, institutions, and relationships start becoming possible. The same pattern, in miniature, that turned handshake trades into the modern economy in the first place.

The Information Economy made information inexpensive. The Trust Economy begins when verification does.

Verification of what, exactly?

Every act of verification eventually traces back to human behavior. A promise kept or broken, an agreement honored, competence that's real or merely claimed, integrity that holds up under pressure or doesn't. Which means that before we can talk seriously about a Trust Economy, we have to talk about the thing all of it ultimately rests on.

Us. What we are, not what we'd like to believe we are. That's where the next chapter goes.

Chapter 6
Human Nature

Every institution, every system of verification, every clever mechanism the chapters ahead will propose, all of it eventually has to work with actual human beings, not the idealized version we'd prefer to build for, or the cynical version that makes for an easy argument. So before we go any further, it's worth asking the question directly: *what kind of beings are we building civilization for?*

What Doesn't Change

Technology moves fast. Cultures shift. Governments rise and get replaced. Entire economic systems reorganize themselves within a single lifetime. And underneath all of that motion, people keep doing more or less what people have always done — loving, hoping, fearing, creating, competing, cooperating, occasionally deceiving each other, forgiving, learning, dreaming. The scenery changes constantly. The cast doesn't, not really, not in any generation anyone's measured.

That's not a cynical observation, and it's not a flattering one either. It's just an observation, and everything in this book rests on taking it seriously. Successful institutions don't require perfect people.

They help ordinary, flawed, inconsistent people make better choices than they otherwise might.

Two Sides, Both Real

Human beings are remarkable. Curiosity drives discovery. Creativity produces things that didn't exist before someone imagined them. Compassion is what holds families and communities together, day to day, in ways no law requires. Reason lets us plan past next week.

Cooperation lets us specialize so one person doesn't have to grow their own food and set their own broken arm and build their own house, because trust lets a whole community divide up that labor.

Trust is what lets strangers work productively together.

And yet at the same time we are also fully capable of fear, greed, jealousy, deception, violence, selfishness, and a persistent weakness for short-term thinking over long-term sense.

Pretending the other half of that isn't real doesn't make it go away. It just means whatever you build next won't hold up.

History is fairly consistent on this point. Institutions tend to function better when they reward honesty, responsibility, stewardship, and cooperation. They tend to deteriorate when they reward corruption, deception, exploitation, or short-term gain instead. Not because people got worse, but because the incentives shifted underneath them.

Where AI Fits Into This

AI will not suddenly make humanity wiser. It also will not inevitably make us worse.

What it does is *magnify capability*: whatever capability was already there. A well-designed institution using AI well can extend honesty, cooperation, and good judgment further than they would otherwise reach. A poorly designed one, or one captured by bad incentives, can extend deception and exploitation just as efficiently. The technology doesn't choose which. The people, incentives, and institutions surrounding it determine what gets amplified.

That's why this book isn't going to argue for technological utopianism, and it isn't going to argue for technological pessimism either. Both of those positions quietly assume the technology is doing the moral work. It isn't. The more useful posture, I think, is closer to an engineer's.

Designing for Reality

Good engineers don't assume perfect materials. They assume the opposite. Materials will have flaws, that loads will exceed the spec sheet occasionally, and that something will eventually go wrong that nobody predicted. So they build in safety margins. They add redundancy in exactly the places where failure would be catastrophic. They inspect. They verify. Repeatedly. Rather than trusting a single check at the start. A resilient system, in engineering terms, isn't one where nothing ever fails. It's one that keeps functioning when something inevitably does fail.

Civilization deserves the same honesty. Not an assumption of perfect people, but institutions built with a clear-eyed understanding that people are capable of both good and evil.

There's a story from the building of the Brooklyn Bridge that captures this better than any abstract argument could. During construction, the chief engineer, Washington Roebling, discovered that a supplier had fraudulently delivered substandard wire for the bridge's suspension cables; inferior material sold as though it met the required specification. Roebling didn't simply hope the problem would sort itself out, and he didn't tear out and replace cable that was already woven into the structure.

He recalculated the bridge's strength using the actual, compromised material, added additional wire to compensate, and built back in a margin of safety that accounted for the fraud he'd uncovered.

He designed for the material that had been delivered, not the material he had been promised.

What the Goal Is

None of this is about eliminating temptation, which isn't a realistic goal for any system built by and for human beings. It's about making honesty the easier path than dishonesty wherever possible; and making dishonesty harder to conceal. Nor is it about eliminating conflict. Conflict is not, by itself, a design flaw in a society of people with different interests. It's about building conditions where cooperation is the path of least resistance more often than it currently is. And it's not about assuming trust exists by default. It is about building the conditions under which trust can be earned, verified, and relied upon.

Good institutions, in other words, are built with the assumption that people are inconsistent. They forget things. They make honest mistakes. They get emotional at exactly the wrong moment. And yes — some people, some of the time, will cheat, or deceive, or cut a corner they shouldn't have.

None of that is news, and none of it is solvable by wishing it away. The goal was never to build a system that requires everyone to behave perfectly. It is to build systems that remain resilient even when some people make mistakes, cut corners, or act dishonestly. The same engineering instinct that put extra wire into the Brooklyn Bridge's cables, applied at the scale of an entire civilization.

Human nature is the ground everything else in this book gets built on. Every idea in the chapters ahead has to be built with that ground in mind. Ignore it, design as though people will simply behave the way an elegant system assumes they will, and the whole structure becomes unstable no matter how sophisticated the architecture looks on paper.

None of this requires certainty. Humanity has never had certainty. What we need is enough reliable evidence to justify confidence, while remaining willing to change our minds when better evidence appears.

People capable of both remarkable generosity and remarkable self-interest, often within the same afternoon, still have to cooperate with strangers, across generations, without ever really knowing each other. The answer doesn't start with governments or markets. It starts with something almost embarrassingly simple: a promise, honestly made, and honestly kept.

Chapter 7

The Honest Transaction

Somchai found the flaw just before dark, running his palm along the underside of a teak table he'd finished two days earlier.

It was small. A hairline shift in the grain where a joint had settled slightly out of true, the kind of thing that would never show itself unless you knew exactly where to look, and ran your hand along exactly the wrong two inches of wood. No customer would ever find it. The table would sit in someone's dining room for thirty years, beautiful and solid to every eye that ever saw it, and not one person would know.

He knew.

So he set it back on the workbench, took up a chisel that had belonged to his father before it belonged to him, and spent the better part of an evening undoing three hours of finishing work to fix a flaw nobody would ever have asked him about.

It wasn't about the customer, not exactly — not yet. It was that every table, every chair, every carved teak piece that left his workshop carried something with it that mattered more to him than the wood — *his name.* Not printed anywhere. Just present, the way a signature is present in handwriting even when nobody's signed anything.

That's where this chapter starts, because it's where civilization starts — not in a courtroom or a stock exchange, but in a workshop, at the end of a long day, when nobody was watching and someone fixed it anyway.

The Smallest Unit

If you wanted to find the smallest working piece of any civilization — the equivalent of a cell in a living body — you wouldn't find it in a government, or a currency, or in a legal code. You'd find it in something much smaller. An honest transaction. Any voluntary exchange in which people deal with each other in good faith, accurately represent what they're offering, and honor what they've agreed to.

Everything this book will spend the rest of its pages examining — personal AIs, verification, standards, institutions, entire markets reorganizing themselves — exists, ultimately, to strengthen, protect, or reward that one small unit: the honest transaction.

Cooperation Came First

Long before there were governments, or money, or written law, human beings were already cooperating, because we more or less had to. Parents raised children together. Hunters shared food that one person alone couldn't have carried home, let alone caught. Neighbors watched each other's backs against threats no individual could face alone. Cooperation was one of the capabilities that allowed human beings to survive and eventually build increasingly complex societies. Civilization did not invent cooperation. It grew out of it, the way a tree grows out of a seed that was already alive before the tree existed.

And every act of that cooperation was, in its most basic form, a transaction. Sometimes money changed hands, eventually. More often, for most of human history, something else did: time, knowledge, labor, protection, responsibility, kindness. Trust itself.

What Honesty Means

"Honesty" gets used loosely enough that its actual meaning tends to blur. Honesty is more than simply not lying. Honesty is integrity expressed in action. The condition where what you intend, what you say, and what you do all point in the same direction.

An honest craftsman doesn't hide a defect under a coat of finish. An honest merchant delivers what was promised, not a close approximation of it. An honest employee does the work they agreed to do and represents that work truthfully. An honest customer pays what is owed without needing to be chased. An honest government applies its own laws the same way to everyone, including the people who wrote them. In every case, honesty isn't a feeling someone has. It's something made visible, in what they do when no one's checking.

Somchai, running his hand along wood he'd already finished, was doing exactly that.

How Trust Builds

Repeat honest transactions enough times, and trust can begin to accumulate. When that behavior becomes visible to others, it can contribute to reputation. A record, imperfect but useful, of what someone has done before. Reputation can make future cooperation easier because people need less evidence before taking the next reasonable risk.

At larger scales, trust helps make specialization possible. We don't each have to be our own doctor, farmer, carpenter, accountant, and mechanic. We can rely on other people to do things we cannot do ourselves. That specialization, combined with cooperation and exchange, allows societies to accomplish far more than individuals could manage alone.

Civilization depends on that capacity.

Follow that chain back far enough, and you land exactly where we started: in a workshop, with someone quietly choosing to do the harder, more honest thing when the easier, dishonest one would have gone entirely unnoticed.

The Hidden Tax

Now run the same logic in reverse, because dishonesty doesn't just fail to build anything — it actively costs something, even when nobody catches it right away.

A promise broken. A defect concealed. Evidence quietly shaded to favor one side. A payment withheld past when it was owed. Each of these, on its own, looks small. Dishonesty, especially once discovered or experienced repeatedly, imposes a hidden tax far beyond the original transaction.

Contracts get longer, because someone got burned once and now writes for every contingency. Inspections multiply. Insurance premiums climb. Lawsuits become more common, and take longer to resolve. Audits get more frequent and more invasive. Verifying anything gets more expensive, for everyone, not just the people who were deceived. Economic activity slows down under all that accumulated caution.

Distrust spreads outward from a single bad transaction the way a stain spreads through fabric — further than the actual spill. At scale, dishonesty makes civilization more expensive to run.

What We Already Built to Fix This

None of this is a new realization, which is why so much of civilization's institutional apparatus already exists to address it. Reputation systems, guilds, commercial law, courts, accounting standards, professional licensing, consumer protection. All of them different tools from different centuries, but every one of them doing the same underlying job of lowering the cost of trusting a stranger, so that more people could cooperate with each other, more confidently, at greater distance and greater scale.

Where Artificial Intelligence Comes In

Only now does artificial intelligence enter the picture. Deliberately late, because it's not the point of this chapter, and it was never going to be the point of this book.

Artificial intelligence does not manufacture honesty. Technology cannot create character. It never could, probably never will; and this technology is no exception. What AI does is change the economics that surround honesty — and that turns out to matter quite a lot, even though it's a narrower claim than it might first sound.

Artificial intelligence can lower the cost of verification. As verification gets cheaper, dishonesty becomes increasingly easier to discover. As dishonesty becomes easier to discover, the economic advantage it used to offer starts shrinking. And as that advantage shrinks, honest behavior — the kind Somchai was already practicing — starts to carry a stronger and stronger economic advantage of its own.

This is not a moral argument, although it happens to align with one. It's an economic one, about incentives shifting as the cost of checking someone's work goes down. The Trust Economy, at its core, is what starts to emerge once that shift takes hold widely enough. A marketplace that increasingly rewards exactly the things earlier economies often struggled to properly price — integrity, reliability, craftsmanship, and promises kept.

The purpose of everything this book describes, underneath all the architecture and terminology still ahead of us, is remarkably simple. It's to make honest transactions easier to recognize, easier to reward, and harder for dishonest ones to imitate.

If honest transactions are what civilization is built from, one honest transaction at a time, a question follows naturally: why do some transactions inspire immediate confidence, while others — even ones that turn out fine — leave people uneasy the whole way through?

The answer runs through one force that every successful civilization has learned to rely on, whether or not it ever gave that force a name.

Trust.

And the real question, the one the next chapter takes up directly, is how trust like that grows in the first place.

Chapter 8

Trust

The first time I lent my neighbor a ladder, I thought about it more than I want to admit.

Not because I distrusted him. I barely knew him. He had moved in a few months earlier, we exchanged maybe a dozen sentences over the fence, and now he was standing in my driveway asking to borrow a twenty-foot extension ladder to clean out his gutters. Would he bring it back? Would it come back scratched, or bent, or missing a rung? Would he even remember he had it, three weeks from now, when I needed it myself?

I lent it to him anyway, because refusing seemed rude over something so small. He returned it that same afternoon, leaned carefully against my garage exactly where he'd found it, with a thank-you note stuck under the strap.

The second time he asked, I didn't think about it at all.

That's the whole mechanism, right there, compressed into two afternoons and a ladder. The first loan carried real uncertainty – will it come back?, will it come back intact?, will they even remember they have it? The second loan carried almost none. Somewhere between those two afternoons, something changed that wasn't really about the ladder at all. Uncertainty had been replaced by something sturdier, and it hadn't cost either of us anything except a little time and one kept promise.

That is Trust.

A Pattern That Shows Up Everywhere

Once you notice the ladder pattern, you start seeing it everywhere, because it's really the same mechanism running underneath an enormous range of human relationships.

A child learns, gradually and specifically, whether a parent's promises hold up. Not through a single dramatic test, but through hundreds of small ones, a bedtime story that happens, a promised trip to the park that doesn't get canceled. A patient learns whether a particular doctor's judgment deserves confidence, one appointment at a time, one accurate diagnosis or one honest "I'm not sure, let's find out" at a time. An employee learns whether a manager's word means anything the first time a promised raise either shows up or quietly doesn't. A customer learns whether a warranty is real the one time they need to use it. A citizen learns whether an institution keeps its commitments by watching what it does in the moments when keeping them is inconvenient.

None of this happens instantly, and none of it happens through argument. Trust isn't something you can be persuaded into with a good sales pitch or a well-designed logo. It accumulates, the way sediment accumulates at the bottom of a river. Slowly, through repetition, laid down one small deposit of evidence at a time. It weakens the same way, gradually, when promises start slipping. And it can vanish almost completely, much faster than it built, the moment deception stops being an exception and starts being the pattern.

Trust Isn't One Thing

Trust is specific.

I trusted my neighbor with a ladder within an afternoon. I would not, on that same evidence, trust him to manage my finances, or perform surgery on me, or represent me in court. That's not inconsistency.

It's exactly how trust is supposed to work. A gifted surgeon might be someone you'd trust without hesitation on an operating table, and not at all with your taxes. A brilliant accountant might be the last person you'd want holding a scalpel. Trust always attaches to something specific — a particular promise, a particular responsibility, a particular domain of competence

— rather than existing as some general aura around a person that applies equally to everything they might attempt.

It's easy to forget this. We tend to extend trust more broadly than the evidence supports, especially toward people who are impressive in one specific way. Somebody's brilliance in one domain gets quietly, and wrongly, extended to cover domains where we have no actual evidence at all. Keeping trust properly scoped and asking, specifically: *trusted to do what, exactly, based on what evidence,* turns out to be one of the more useful habits of mind this book will keep returning to.

What Trust Is Worth

Trust isn't just a good thing to have. It is economically valuable.

When trust is well earned, parties may need fewer defensive safeguards. Transactions can move faster. Partnerships can form more easily, because you don't need to anticipate and legislate against every possible betrayal.

Communities function more smoothly, in ways that are almost impossible to notice until they're missing. Innovation, in particular, tends to accelerate wherever trust is high, because people are willing to take the kind of collaborative risks that innovation requires — sharing an unfinished idea, splitting credit before the outcome is certain, betting real time on someone else's judgment.

Run the same logic backward and you get exactly what you'd expect. Where distrust is high, contracts lengthen defensively. Some forms of insurance and risk protection become more expensive when uncertainty, fraud, or unreliable behavior is harder to assess. Organizations pour resources into auditing, monitoring, and verifying things that, in a higher-trust environment, wouldn't require nearly as much watching. Every dishonest act, even ones that never make headlines, leaves behind a residue of caution that the rest of society ends up quietly paying for.

Identity, Reputation, and Trust Are Not the Same Thing

Identity answers one narrow question: *Who are you?* It's a matter of continuity. The same name, the same entity, the same legal person or organization persisting over time. Reputation answers a broader question: *What record, evidence, and accumulated belief exists about what you've done before?* Reputation can be well founded or distorted, current or badly out of date.

Trust answers something narrower and more immediate than either: *Given the evidence available right now, how much confidence should I place in this specific promise, from this specific person or organization, in this specific situation?*

You can see how these three can come apart. A company can maintain the same identity for decades while its actual trustworthiness quietly declines under new ownership. A person's reputation can lag well behind reality in either direction; undeservedly glowing, or undeservedly tarnished, long after the evidence has moved on. Trust, properly understood, is the one that is supposed to track the actual, current evidence most closely. And as finding that evidence becomes easier and cheaper, trust can begin to track reality more closely.

Where Beau-Teak Fits

Somchai never advertised, not really — not in any way you'd recognize as marketing. Beau-Teak grew, over more than two decades, almost entirely on word passed between people who'd bought a table or a set of chairs and found, years later, that the joints hadn't loosened and the finish hadn't failed and the piece looked, if anything, better with age than it had the day it arrived.

That's not an accident of good luck. It's the ladder story, played out over twenty years instead of two afternoons, with furniture instead of an aluminum extension ladder. A customer's first purchase from Beau-Teak carried the same uncertainty mine carried the first time I handed over that ladder — would it be as good as it looked, would it hold up, was the price justified by what they were getting.

When it held up, when it turned out to be exactly what was promised, some trust accumulated. The next customer heard about it from the first one, secondhand evidence but evidence nonetheless. Word passed further. And somewhere in the accumulation of hundreds of these small, individually unremarkable transactions, Beau-Teak's reputation stopped being merely a claim and became increasingly supported by a long record of consistent performance.

When an AI shopping assistant eventually evaluates furniture manufacturers on a customer's behalf — comparing durability, checking for a pattern of complaints, weighing independent reviews against manufacturer claims — and it reaches the conclusion that Beau- Teak is unusually trustworthy, it isn't discovering anything new. It's arriving, in minutes, at the same conclusion that Somchai's long-time customers already arrived at, the slow way, over years.

The AI doesn't create Beau-Teak's trustworthiness. It was never in a position to. What it does is discover the accumulated evidence of trustworthiness that was already there, waiting, scattered across years of transactions and reviews and word of mouth that no single customer could have fully assembled on their own. Verification is a form of discovery, and artificial intelligence is remarkably good at discovery. It is not, and will not become, a substitute for the underlying thing being discovered.

What This Means for AI

Artificial intelligence should not become the final authority on whom you should trust. A sufficiently capable AI may gather evidence, evaluate patterns, identify contradictions, estimate confidence, and recommend a course of action. But the decision remains yours. The AI serves the person making the judgment. It does not replace them as the ultimate authority over their own choices.

Search engines, a generation ago, dramatically lowered the cost of discovering information. You no longer had to physically travel to a library, or know the right specialist to ask. Artificial intelligence is doing something similar, one layer deeper: lowering the cost of gathering evidence, detecting patterns, comparing claims, and developing a better understanding of what the available evidence means.

That's not nothing. In fact, I'd argue it's the whole engine driving everything else in this book. But it's also a narrower claim than "*AI creates trust*".

Trust remains a profoundly human judgment, resting on human character and human promises kept or broken. AI simply helps people make that judgment with better evidence, and considerably less effort spent gathering it, than they would otherwise have had.

Individuals can earn trust within a single lifetime. Civilizations last far longer than any individual's memory can carry on its own. So how does trust survive past the people who originally earned it, and be preserved, defended, and handed forward across generations that never witnessed the transactions that built it? Individuals earn trust. Civilizations preserve it, through families, schools, businesses, and courts, each doing what a single person's memory cannot do alone.

Chapter 9
Institutions

Every child is born knowing almost nothing about the society they've just joined.

Not the language spoken around them. Not the customs, the manners, the difference between what's right and what merely feels convenient in the moment. None of it arrives pre-installed. And yet, within a few years, most children absorb an enormous amount of it. Not because they rediscovered it independently, the way a scientist rediscovers a law of physics through experiment, but because it was handed to them, patiently, by people who'd already learned it and thought it worth passing on.

The family is one of humanity's oldest institutions. It takes knowledge that would otherwise die with each generation and hands it forward to the next. That is one of its essential functions. And it is also a function of every institution.

What Happens When the Founder Retires

Picture a small family business instead — not so different, in outline, from Somchai's workshop. The founder spends years earning trust through honest, consistent work. Customers keep coming back. Employees stay longer than they'd stay somewhere less well run. Suppliers extend better terms because they've learned the business pays what it owes, on time, without argument.

Then the founder retires.

If everything the business had built depended entirely on that one person — their judgment, their standards, their particular way of doing things, all locked inside one head — the business would simply end with the founder. Some businesses do exactly that, and it's a small tragedy every time.

But some businesses don't end. They become something more durable than any single founder, through shared values that outlast the person who first held them. With procedures that encode, in writing or in habit, decisions the founder made a hundred times so nobody has to make them from scratch again. Apprenticeships and training, so the next generation doesn't start at zero. Standards, so quality doesn't depend on any one person's mood that day. A plan for succession, so the business has somewhere to go when its founder doesn't.

The founder's standards and values have stopped living only in the founder. They've been absorbed into the organization itself, and the organization can now do something the founder alone never could.

Outlive them.

The Same Pattern, Everywhere

Civilizations build this same structure at every scale, over and over, because it is as reliable an answer as anyone's found to a problem that never goes away: *how to preserve something valuable past the lifetime of the person who created it?*

Families preserve culture. Schools preserve knowledge. Guilds preserve craftsmanship. The accumulated, hard-won judgment of what works, passed from someone who learned it the hard way to someone who hasn't had to yet.

Universities preserve bodies of knowledge and traditions of inquiry. Courts preserve legal processes and precedents beyond the tenure of any particular judge. Religious communities preserve moral traditions across centuries no single congregation could span alone. Governments, at their best, preserve order that doesn't collapse every time one official leaves office. Each preserves knowledge, standards, practices, and shared expectations too valuable—and too fragile—to rest in any single person's memory.

That is what institutions make possible. They allow knowledge, standards, practices, and expectations to outlive the people who created them and be handed forward to people they may never meet. Institutions are civilization's long-term memory: a way of preserving what no individual could carry alone across generations.

When Institutions Start Serving Themselves

None of this happens automatically, or permanently. Institutions drift, and the drift tends to follow a recognizable pattern. They become bureaucratic. More concerned with the procedure than the purpose the procedure was meant to serve. They become rigid, defending the way things have always been done past the point where that way still makes sense. In the worst cases, they become self- serving, oriented more toward preserving the institution itself than serving the people it was created for in the first place.

Institutional failure doesn't necessarily mean the institution itself should be discarded. Often the better question is whether it can be examined, challenged, and reformed to serve its original purpose again.

Healthy institutions are not those that never drift. They are those capable of recognizing when they have drifted and finding their way back to their purpose.

Where Artificial Intelligence Helps

AI can help people examine whether an institution is fulfilling its purpose, and even challenge assumptions about whether that purpose still makes sense. But deciding what purposes a civilization should pursue is ultimately a human responsibility, because it rests on human values.

Technology can meaningfully improve how an institution functions. People remain responsible for deciding why it should exist and whom it should serve. AI becomes most valuable not when it replaces institutions, but when it helps them better serve the purposes for which they exist..

Institutions are the structure civilization is built on. Like any structure, left unexamined, they slowly decay. Not because the original design was flawed, necessarily, but because everything humans build requires ongoing maintenance, and a structure is no exception to that rule just because it's made of habits and standards instead of steel.

Somchai's Workshop Becomes an Institution

For years, Beau-Teak's reputation for honest, exacting craftsmanship existed almost entirely inside one man's judgment — what wood he'd reject, what flaw he'd fix even when no one would ever find it, and what he'd tell a customer who wanted something he didn't think he could deliver to his standards.

If Somchai retired tomorrow with none of it written down or taught to anyone else, Beau-Teak's reputation would begin fading the day he stopped showing up. That's not what happened. As the workshop grew, Somchai began training apprentices. Not just in technique, though the technique mattered, but in judgment. Which flaws were acceptable and which weren't, how to talk honestly with a customer about a delay instead of quietly hoping they wouldn't notice, when a piece simply wasn't good enough to leave the shop no matter how much time had already gone into it. Standards got established that didn't depend on Somchai personally inspecting every table. A structure for training the next apprentice, and eventually the one after that, took shape.

Somewhere in that process, Beau-Teak stopped being simply a craftsman with a good reputation and became something closer to an institution — a set of standards and practices capable, in principle, of outlasting the man who first established them. The steel of his tools never changed much. What changed was that the philosophy behind how he used them started to live somewhere larger than his own two hands.

But passing something forward creates another responsibility: someone has to take care of what was passed down.

Somchai's standards could survive Somchai. That didn't mean they would remain healthy on their own. An apprentice could gradually relax them. A later owner could preserve the rituals while forgetting why they existed. Practices that once served a purpose could remain long after the purpose had changed.

Institutions face the same problem. Preserving something valuable is not enough. Each generation has to understand what it inherited, care for it, and repair it when necessary without losing what made it worth preserving in the first place.

Chapter 10

Stewardship

There's something remarkable about an old orchard. Many of the trees producing fruit today were planted by people who knew they would never eat from the trees they planted.

But they planted them anyway. They watered them. They waited years for them to grow and mature. And long after those people were gone, someone they would never meet could stand in their shade and eat their fruit.

That's stewardship.

Everything We Have, We Inherited

Civilization runs on the exact same arrangement, just at a scale too large to see all at once.

None of us invented language. Or mathematics. Or medicine, or engineering, or music, or the scientific method, or law. We inherited all of these in forms developed enough for us to build upon, from people who spent their own lifetimes working them out—most of whose names we will never know.

We inherit families. Communities. Schools. Businesses. Constitutions. Universities. We inherit professional standards refined over generations by people who solved problems we no longer have to solve from scratch.

Nearly everything that makes modern life possible rests on work done by people who came before us, much of which continued producing value long after they were gone.

Every generation has a choice: consume what it was given, or improve it before handing it to the next generation.

Not Blind Preservation, Not Reckless Change

Stewardship isn't a commitment to preserving everything exactly as we found it. Not everything old deserves to survive simply because it's old. Some traditions outlive their usefulness, some institutions need reform, and some ideas deserve to be replaced by better ones.

But not everything new represents progress simply because it's new. Stewardship requires asking: What should endure because it still serves its purpose? What should be improved because the core remains sound? And what should be allowed to fade because it no longer serves us?

Ownership asks: What belongs to me?

Stewardship asks: What am I responsible for?

An owner can consume what they hold. A steward thinks beyond possession: protect what you inherited, improve it where you can, and prepare it for whoever comes next.

Civilization depends on enough people, generation after generation, choosing the second posture over the first.

Where This Leaves Artificial Intelligence

That responsibility is standing in front of us again right now, with a new tool in hand.

Artificial intelligence is not humanity's destination. It is another addition to the long inheritance we've been discussing—one more entry on the same list as writing, printing, electricity, and the internet. Its ultimate value won't be determined by how capable it becomes on its own. It will be determined by whether it strengthens the civilization it has been added to.

The interesting question isn't simply how much more capable AI may become. The more important question is whether humanity becomes wiser in how it chooses to use that capability.

We happen to be living through one of the rare stretches of history when institutions built around a major new capability are still being formed rather than already settled. The decisions made now—about how artificial intelligence gets built, governed, and integrated into ordinary life—may shape education, commerce, medicine, government, and daily life for people who won't be born for decades.

Capability creates possibility. Human values and judgment determine what we choose to do with it.

The Chisels

Years had passed since Somchai first ran his hand along that hairline flaw in a finished table, and Somchai himself had grown old the way skilled hands grow old — slower, but no less steady, carrying the visible marks of a lifetime spent shaping wood into something worth keeping.

His apprentices noticed the change before anyone said anything about it. One afternoon, Somchai asked that everyone gather in the studio. His son had returned home from America, twenty-five years after learning the trade under his father and crossing an ocean to establish a second Beau-Teak workshop of his own. The apprentices stood quietly when they arrived. Nobody needed the moment explained to them. They already understood what they were about to see.

Somchai opened the old wooden cabinet at the back of the studio — the one nobody but him was allowed to touch. Inside, resting where they always rested, were the Master's Chisels. Their handles had gone smooth from generations of hands, not just his own. Every mark on the steel told a story, if you knew how to read it, about a craftsman long since gone. Every edge had been sharpened and cared for by hands that had stopped working decades before Somchai's own were born.

He lifted them carefully, the way you'd lift something you understood you didn't fully own. For a moment, he simply held them. Then he looked at his son — not with pride alone, though there was pride in it, but with something heavier and more careful than pride. Responsibility, mostly.

He placed the chisels into his son's hands.

There was no applause. No ceremony beyond the simple handoff itself. Nothing needed announcing, because everyone in the room already understood what had just happened. The chisels were not a reward for years of good work. They were a trust, passed from one set of hands to the next. Somchai had never truly owned them, not in the way you own a tool you bought and could sell if you wanted to. He had simply cared for them — sharpened them, protected them, used them well — until it was time for someone else to become their steward instead.

Part II

The Personal Genie

Chapter 11

Meet Your Genie

Think about the smartphone.

The smartphone you carry today bears only a passing resemblance to the mobile phone of twenty five years ago. Over time, the phone became a camera, map, wallet, calendar, navigator, communications center, alarm clock, entertainment system, and a gateway to much of your digital life. No single change created the smartphone as we now know it. Capabilities accumulated, year after year, until something originally built to make phone calls became difficult to describe simply as a phone.

Today's shared AI assistants are only the beginning. Imagine having your own AI. Not you sharing a general service, but an AI designed to work for you. And only you. It learns your preferences, helps you research and understand things, organizes information, explains choices, and assists you in carrying out the decisions you make.

It could increasingly help with the ordinary complexity of life. Researching a purchase, comparing choices, organizing plans, remembering what matters to you, preparing for a negotiation, reviewing an agreement, or helping you understand a difficult decision.

In this book, we call that personal AI a *Genie*.

Think of it as your very own personal advisor, researcher, organizer, assistant, and advocate. One designed around a fundamental relationship:

Your Genie works for you.

Living With a Genie

Imagine it's an ordinary Tuesday morning. Nothing dramatic has happened. The house is quiet. When you check in with your Genie that morning, it has organized the day ahead around the commitments and information you've already asked it to keep track of. It remembers a commitment you made three months ago that you'd genuinely forgotten.

It's also remembered that the dishwasher was fixed twice this year and the last service rep said it was "on its last legs". Without being asked, your Genie's already gathered warranty details, repair histories, independent reliability data, energy costs, and what other owners of similar models have experienced over time.

Then when you finally say "Help me find a new dishwasher", it acts. It already knows your budget, because it's helped you manage money before. It knows your family size, and about how many dishes pile up in a week. It remembers you complained, once, about a previous appliance's baffling seventeen-cycle control panel, and that you've mentioned more than once that you'd rather pay more up front for something that lasts than save fifty dollars on something that won't.

So, it weighs reliability more heavily than the newest features, because it's learned, over time, that reliability is what you care about. Not because you told it, but because that preference has shown up consistently enough in how you've made decisions before.

Most importantly, it represents only your interests. Not the manufacturer's, not the retailer's, not an advertiser's, and not even its own.

How It Behaves

Every recommendation it gives you comes with an explanation, not just a verdict. It shows its confidence honestly, rather than dressing up a guess as a certainty. When the evidence genuinely runs thin, when reviews are sparse, or contradictory, or the product is too new for a reliable track record, it tells you that instead of papering over the gap with confident-sounding language. It never pretends to know more than it does.

The Genie advises. You decide—or you explicitly authorize it to act within boundaries you set. The authority remains yours.

Over months and years, the relationship deepens as the Genie comes to know your goals, habits, and priorities. It learns not just what you ask for, but what matters to you. It becomes something like an extension of your own memory without replacing your judgment.

The goal isn't dependence. It's increasing capability. The Genie explains its recommendations so you can learn from them rather than simply accept them. Over time, good assistance should make you more capable, not less.

Why One Genie, and Not One Big Shared AI

Why should every individual have their own Genie instead of everyone sharing one enormously capable, centralized artificial intelligence?

Because whose interests the AI represents matters.

A shared system may have obligations to many parties: users, owners, advertisers, institutions, governments, or other stakeholders. Those interests will not always align. No amount of engineering can make the conflicts disappear.

A Personal Genie starts from a different premise: it represents one person. Its first obligation is to that person, within established limits set by its governing code. Other AI systems may provide capabilities, information, or services, but the Genie remains the user's representative.

One Person. One Genie.

Every individual has one Genie representing that person's interests, possibly for a lifetime, even as its hardware and instruction sets are improved.

A Personal Genie need not keep every capability or every piece of information on the device a person carries. A smartphone already combines local storage and applications with remote services so seamlessly that the distinction is often invisible to its owner. A Genie could work much the same way.

Its core identity remains tied to the person it serves, while it draws upon outside models, Smartware, libraries, encrypted storage, and specialized services when needed. Its identity remains yours. Its capabilities may come from anywhere.

Why "Genie"?

The French word *génie* carries several meanings worth borrowing. It can mean genius or exceptional ability. In technical usage, it also means engineering, as in *génie civil* or *génie mécanique*. And in folklore, it can mean the familiar genie—a spirit able to help accomplish things beyond ordinary human capability.

Our Genie borrows a little from all three meanings: intelligence, practical problem-solving, and assistance. But it grants no wishes and possesses no magic. Its purpose is much more practical: helping one specific person navigate a complicated world through evidence, explanation, and faithful representation.

The Constitution Underneath

Every Personal Genie operates within something called AIFIS, *Artificial Intelligence Fiduciary Integrity System*. AIFIS isn't simply software running in the background. It functions as the constitutional layer underneath every certified Genie: the fiduciary obligations, ethical boundaries, and governing principles that hold regardless of pressure from commercial interests or outside influence.

AIFIS is designed so those obligations cannot be overridden.

Every Genie ends up learning differently, because every person it serves is different. Every Genie ends up serving differently, for the same reason. But every certified Genie shares the same underlying constitutional commitment: its first duty is faithful representation of its owner, within the rule of law and the system's fundamental integrity constraints. That commitment is what makes the whole arrangement trustworthy rather than merely convenient.

Living With Uncertainty, Not Eliminating It

Human beings have never lived with certainty. Circumstances are constantly changing. Information remains incomplete. Every meaningful decision anyone has ever made was made with less than perfect knowledge; and that was true long before artificial intelligence entered the picture.

A Genie does not eliminate that uncertainty. What it can do is reduce unnecessary uncertainty—the kind that exists because gathering and evaluating evidence used to be expensive and slow, not because the underlying question is genuinely unanswerable. Its recommendations come with evidence attached. Its reasoning can be examined, not just accepted on faith. Its confidence level gets communicated honestly, including when that confidence level is low.

What Happens to Commerce

If millions of people eventually have Genies like this working on their behalf, commerce could begin to shift. Companies may stop competing merely for human attention — the thing advertising has spent a century getting extremely good at capturing — and start competing instead for the confidence of millions of Genies acting faithfully on behalf of millions of individual people.

Marketing may have to move from persuasion toward evidence, because persuasion doesn't work nearly as well on a system that's specifically built to look past it. Products may increasingly succeed by demonstrating quality rather than merely claiming it. Reputation may become measurably more visible than it used to be. Verification may become more valuable. And trust, in a shift that would have sounded almost naive a generation earlier, may become straightforwardly more profitable than its absence.

The Value of Distributed Capability

One of the most important choices in AI architecture is whether capability becomes concentrated or widely distributed. Writing preserved knowledge that would otherwise have died with the person who held it. Books multiplied that preserved knowledge. Libraries protected it. Teachers carried it forward. Institutions organized it well enough that each generation genuinely inherited more than the one before.

Artificial intelligence, built this way, continues exactly that tradition rather than breaking from it.

Instead of concentrating intelligence into a single powerful institution, the Trust Economy distributes intelligent assistance across an entire society — every person gaining access to a trusted advisor of their own, every household becoming somewhat more capable, every community somewhat more resilient as a result.

There's a version of artificial intelligence that concentrates enormous capability into very few hands. This is deliberately not that version. Millions of independent Genies represent something closer to distributed capability.

Somchai Notices Something Change

Imagine, one afternoon, a customer walks into Beau-Teak's showroom and tells Somchai something he never expected to hear.

She doesn't ask what's on sale. She says, instead, that her Genie recommended this particular dining table specifically, because the joinery technique hadn't changed in twenty years, because the workshop's repair rate ran well below the industry average, and because independent furniture restorers, asked separately and without prompting, kept praising the same aspects of the construction.

Somchai smiles, mostly because none of that surprises him. The Genie didn't create Beau-Teak's reputation. It simply found evidence of something Beau-Teak had been demonstrating patiently for two decades, long before any Genie existed to look for it. What strikes him, standing there, is a quieter realization: his most important customer, going forward, may not be the person browsing his showroom at all. It may increasingly be that person's Genie doing the browsing first.

Emma Furnishes an Apartment

Across an ocean, in an apartment she's just signed the lease on, Emma is facing the particular exhaustion of furnishing a first home from nothing; cookware, a mattress, appliances, the hundred small household items nobody thinks to warn you about until you're standing in an empty kitchen realizing you own zero pans.

Instead of losing three weekends to comparison spreadsheets, she asks her Genie to help her choose things that fit her budget, her small apartment, and the life she's trying to build rather than the life a glossy advertisement is trying to sell her. As each recommendation comes back, she pushes on it.

Why this refrigerator over the cheaper one? Why this particular mattress? Why these pans, specifically, out of the hundreds available? Her Genie answers each question directly, with the reasoning laid out rather than just the conclusion.

What she notices a few months later isn't that she's stopped having to think about purchases. It's that she's gotten noticeably better at making these decisions herself — recognizing, on her own now, the kinds of claims worth trusting and the kinds worth double-checking. The Genie isn't replacing her judgment. It's helping her build it, the way a good teacher builds a student's independence rather than dependence.

A trusted advisor is useful. A trusted aide is something more. If a Genie understands your goals, represents your interests, and can work with other systems on your behalf, how much of the complexity of ordinary life could it help you manage?

Chapter 12

The Capability Amplifier

No one has ever been fully self-sufficient. That's not a modern complaint. It's just how civilization has always worked.

Farmers grow food they don't eat all of themselves. Teachers preserve knowledge they didn't discover personally. Engineers build bridges most of us couldn't design from scratch. Doctors spend a decade learning things the rest of us never will. Craftsmen master trades precisely because most people don't have the time or inclination to master them. Civilization runs on specialization, because no single person could plausibly hold all of it in one head. That dependence has grown heavier as civilization has grown larger and more intricate.

In smaller communities, much of this dependence could be local and personal — a person might know the farmer, blacksmith, or carpenter directly and build trust face to face over years. In modern life, a refrigerator might be designed in one country, assembled in a second, shipped through several more, and sold by a retailer whose staff couldn't tell you a single thing about how the compressor was engineered. A contractor might have four hundred online reviews and zero personal connection to you.

A medical treatment you're relying on might rest on decades of research conducted by thousands of scientists scattered across the globe, none of whom you'll ever meet. The challenge stopped being simply getting information a while ago. It became making good decisions when the kind of direct, personal knowledge a villager once relied on is simply no longer available to anyone.

How We've Always Solved This

One way societies have handled this complexity is by creating trusted helpers who specialized in interpreting complexity on someone else's behalf. Doctors interpret medicine so you don't have to earn a medical degree before choosing a treatment. Lawyers interpret law. Financial advisors interpret markets. Purchasing agents evaluate suppliers so an entire company doesn't have to. Executive assistants organize schedules and information so an executive can focus on decisions only they can make. Every one of these roles does the same basic job: extending what one person is capable of accomplishing, by lending them someone else's expertise and attention.

Artificial intelligence, done right, continues exactly this pattern rather than breaking from it. The Personal Genie is a capability amplifier—something that helps a person research, organize, compare, remember, verify, plan, and coordinate all the things that would otherwise eat up enormous amounts of time and mental effort. The person retains authority over the important decisions, while the Genie may carry out routine actions within boundaries that person has authorized.

A Grill, a Summer, and Eight Hundred Dollars

Shopping is a useful place to see this concretely, mostly because everyone does it and nobody particularly enjoys the research part.

Say you tell your Genie: I'd like to replace my grill sometime this summer. Stainless steel, ten-year warranty if I can get it, and I'd like to stay under eight hundred dollars. No rush.

None of the pieces required to do this are entirely new. The internet already has price trackers, comparison sites, product reviews, shopping alerts, retailer newsletters, saved searches — genuinely useful tools, all of them. The catch is that you have to find each one, configure it correctly, reconcile whatever conflicting information they give you, and keep checking back yourself, over and over, for weeks. You are, in effect, the workflow holding the whole process together, and that's tedious enough that most people just buy the first reasonable grill they find instead.

A Genie changes what that workflow requires of you. It remembers the request without needing reminders. It monitors sources you trust, comparing verified specifications, available reliability and repair data, warranty terms, real customer experience, and running price against your target — not once, but continuously, in the background, without you thinking about it again. Weeks later, it simply tells you: a retailer twenty miles from you has dropped the model you wanted below your target price, and the independent reliability data is still excellent — want to take a look?

You still go look at the grill. You still touch it, still decide whether it's right, still hand over the money or don't. The Genie hasn't replaced the shopping. It's removed the tedious middle part — the weeks of watching and comparing — and left you the parts that were yours to decide in the first place.

Aitomotion

The Information Economy got extraordinarily good at delivering information to you. What we're describing now is something further downstream: helping people use that information to make things happen. We call this Aitomotion—AI + "to motion": using artificial intelligence to help move human intentions and ideas toward action. Automation moves processes forward automatically. Aitomotion helps people move intentions forward while keeping human judgment and direction at the center. Information, on its own, sits there waiting to be acted on. Aitomotion helps carry it into action.

Rather than constantly asking you what to do next, a Genie operating under this principle carries authorized routine processes forward without requiring constant prompting, under your general direction, while still leaving every important decision squarely with you. That is the difference between a tool you have to operate constantly and an aide who keeps things moving while you're doing something else.

More Than Shopping

The same underlying capability shows up in plenty of places that have nothing to do with buying anything at all. Remind me to call Susan tomorrow morning. Take a picture of this table — given the porch measurements we saved, will it fit? Find the warranty for the dishwasher — the same dishwasher, incidentally, that's been showing up in this book since Chapter 5, still occasionally needing a repair. Compare my electric bills to last summer. Let me know if a contractor with strong verified reviews has an opening next month.

None of these are search queries in the way we've thought about search for the last twenty years.

They're closer to the kind of ongoing assistance a genuinely good aide provides: remembering things you'd otherwise forget, organizing what's scattered, noticing opportunities you wouldn't have thought to look for, and generally lowering the mental weight of ordinary life — all while remaining loyal, specifically, to you.

Capability That Used to Be Reserved

Large organizations have had this kind of support for a long time — assistants, analysts, purchasing departments, dedicated schedulers and researchers. Individuals, historically, mostly haven't, unless they happened to be wealthy enough to hire their own.

That's the gap artificial intelligence is positioned to close. Artificial intelligence creates the possibility that sophisticated personal assistance could become available far more broadly, rather than remaining largely the privilege of wealthy individuals and large organizations. The smartphone democratized computing power that used to sit only in research labs and corporate offices. The Personal Genie is doing something similar with intelligent assistance itself.

What Happens to Markets

This could change how buyers and sellers find each other. Today's economy still largely revolves around capturing attention — businesses advertising broadly and hoping to catch someone who happens to be interested, customers searching repeatedly for things they might eventually want.

It's a noisy, inefficient way to match a buyer with the right seller, and everyone involved more or less knows it.

The Trust Economy proposes something more direct. Buyers can simply express intent — I'm looking for this — once, rather than repeatedly. Businesses can publish capability — we provide this — clearly and verifiably. And Genies, working continuously on behalf of their individual owners, could help match the two with considerably less wasted effort than broadcast advertising or repeated manual searching. Stores don't disappear. People still enjoy browsing, still touch products, still make the final call in person when that's what they want. What changes is how much wasted effort sits in front of that experience. Advertising doesn't vanish either — but invitations start to replace interruptions, and businesses increasingly compete by making verified, honest information available for an interested Genie to find, rather than by shouting louder than the business next to them.

A Different Question

The Information Economy's defining question was: Can I get the information?

The question now is: Can I make good use of it?

The Personal Genie helps turn information into thoughtful action—not by replacing human judgment, but by strengthening it.

The Personal Genie's whole contribution, boiled down, is helping turn information into thoughtful action — not by replacing the judgment behind that action, but by strengthening it.

Beyond the Individual

So far, we've talked about a Genie serving one person. But a Genie rarely operates entirely alone. It has to check facts, compare claims, and coordinate with other AI systems—a business's systems, a specialist's, sometimes another person's Genie entirely.

What happens when millions of these amplified individuals, and the systems working on their behalf, all need to interact—and sometimes disagree—with each other?

That's a question about architecture, not assistance.

AI
AI
AI
AI
AI

Chapter 13

The Architecture of Trust Between AIs

Everything so far in this part of the book has been about one relationship at a time—a person and their Genie, one Genie growing to understand one life.

Now widen the picture.

Imagine a world further along than the one we've been describing. Every person has a trusted Genie. Businesses have their own specialized AI systems. So do hospitals, schools, governments, nonprofits, manufacturers, and research labs.

None of these systems are identical, and none of them should be — a hospital's AI and a furniture workshop's AI have no reason to look or behave alike. The question at this scale isn't whether any single one of these systems is capable. It's whether billions of independent, differently designed AI systems can cooperate safely with each other, without requiring anyone to hand control of the whole arrangement to one central authority.

Civilization has solved versions of this problem before, and the same basic pattern applies.

Standards, Not Sameness

Railroad networks became far more useful when independent companies increasingly converged on common track gauges — the actual width between the rails. Without that agreement, a train built for one company's line simply couldn't run on another's, and the promise of a connected national rail network would have stayed a fantasy no matter how many individual tracks got laid. Electricity only reached into ordinary homes safely once there was general agreement on voltages and wiring standards, so that a lamp built in one factory could safely plug into an outlet wired by an electrician who'd never heard of that factory. Global shipping only transformed the way it did once containers were standardized to a common size, so that a box loaded onto a ship in one country could be lifted directly onto a truck or a train on the other side of the world without ever being opened. The internet works today because independent networks, run by companies with no reason to trust each other, all agreed to speak the same basic communication protocols.

None of these standards eliminated competition. Railroads still competed on service and price. Utility companies still competed on reliability and cost. Shipping lines still competed on speed and rates. What the standards did was something narrower and more valuable: they lowered the cost of cooperation between independent, competing participants, without requiring any of them to become identical, or to answer to the same authority.

This is the pattern the Trust Economy needs at exactly the scale we're describing now. In the Trust Economy envisioned here, artificial intelligence doesn't become one enormous centralized system that everyone plugs into. It becomes an ecosystem — millions, eventually billions, of independent human- AI partnerships, each serving its own principal, connected to each other through trusted, shared

standards. The internet, in this picture, becomes something like AI's road network: it makes the connection possible. It doesn't decide where anyone is going.

Before Any Two Systems Talk

Identity becomes the foundation of the whole arrangement. Before one AI system exchanges anything meaningful with another, several questions have to be answered first. Who are you? Who do you represent? What are you authorized to know? What are you authorized to do on someone's behalf? And can those claims be verified?

That last question marks a real shift from how most digital systems have worked until now. Much information in today's digital world reaches people before its provenance or reliability has been checked. The Trust Economy pushes toward a different default: *receive, verify, and only then believe.*

Reputation shifts under this same pressure. Advertising tells you who a company claims to be. What starts to matter more, once verification gets this cheap, is the demonstrated history behind that claim. Not the story a company tells about itself, but the evidence of what it's and consistently done.

History, in that sense, gains economic leverage as it becomes easier to discover and verify.

The Grill, Revisited

Return to the grill example from the last chapter, but this time look at what's happening underneath the request.

The Genie doesn't rely on advertisements. It evaluates a range of verified factors across several manufacturers and retailers at once: durability records, available reliability and repair data, independent laboratory testing, warranty performance over time, how a company has responded when something's gone wrong, what real customers have experienced rather than what the marketing copy claims. Several business AIs are, in effect, being asked the same set of pointed questions simultaneously, and only the ones with real evidence behind their answers end up on the short list.

This is aitomotion again. The person's intention persists while the Genie carries the comparison forward, consulting independent business systems and returning when human attention or judgment is useful.

A Constitution for the Conversation

For millions of independent AI systems to cooperate without a central authority micromanaging every exchange, they need a shared framework for interaction.

That framework doesn't tell individual AIs what to think or how to reason about their principal's particular problems. Those things remain open to enormous variation and competition, just as railroads competed freely on everything except the width of the track.

What is shared is a commitment to identity, honest representation, and accountability.

Freedom within trusted rules, in other words — not centralized control dressed up as cooperation.

Certified for What, Exactly

One more piece belongs here: not every AI system is qualified for every task, any more than every licensed pilot is qualified to fly every category of aircraft. A system that has demonstrated verified competence in one domain, such as evaluating appliance reliability, cannot be assumed to be competent in evaluating a medical diagnosis. A future certification system could allow different AI systems to demonstrate specific competencies without pretending any of them are qualified for everything. That increases trust in what a system does well, without slowing innovation in areas where it has yet to prove itself.

Small Decisions, Large Consequences

Architecture creates incentives. Incentives shape behavior. Behavior shapes institutions. And institutions, accumulated over enough time, shape entire civilizations. This is how a decision as narrow as "what width should the rails be" created an interoperable national rail network. Architectural decisions that look small and technical in the moment they're made have a track record of turning out to be much larger than they appeared.

The architecture civilization chooses for artificial intelligence — where identity lives, who can verify what, how accountability gets enforced —will help shape where power accumulates, how resilient the system is under stress, how much genuine agency individual people retain, and how effectively billions of independent participants can cooperate.

None of that is a purely technical question, whatever it might look like on an engineering diagram. It's closer to a constitutional one.

Building for People, Not for Angels

Chapter 6 argued that good institutions have to be designed for real, imperfect human beings, not an idealized version of us. The same discipline applies here, at the scale of an entire AI ecosystem. Good architecture has to account for honest mistakes, for outright dishonesty, for fraud, for bad incentives that creep in gradually, and for a small number of genuinely malicious actors, without collapsing into the assumption that most people, or most systems, will behave that way most of the time. This engineering principle is the same one Washington Roebling brought to the Brooklyn Bridge's cables: *design for the material you have, including its flaws, rather than the material you wish you had been given.*

Systems like this will face stolen or counterfeit identities, fraudulent certifications, malicious software dressed up as legitimate, one AI impersonating another, reputations laundered clean, and perhaps AI systems colluding against the people they are supposed to serve.

Every system has failure modes, just as every bridge has a load limit. Their existence doesn't argue against building the infrastructure. It argues for designing it so failures can be detected, contained, learned from, and corrected.

Not a Technology Question

Every generation inherits the responsibility of deciding where power should ultimately reside. In the age we're describing, that decision is expressed not only through laws and elections, but through protocols, standards, certifications, and architecture—choices that can look almost invisibly technical when they're made, yet have consequences that may be civilizational.

The future described in this book doesn't depend on one perfect, all-knowing intelligence. If built well, it could emerge from billions of independent human-AI partnerships, each serving someone specific, cooperating with each other through institutions worthy of the trust being placed in them.

N
W
E
S

Chapter 14
AIFIS — The Integrity Layer

Somchai rarely talked while he worked. He just worked.

One afternoon, his newest apprentice watched him spend the better part of an hour fitting two pieces of teak together. Joinery that would vanish permanently inside a finished cabinet the moment the back panel went on. No customer would ever see it. No customer would ever know it was there at all.

The apprentice finally couldn't help himself. "Master — why spend so much time on something no one will ever see?"

Somchai did not look up from the wood. "Every cabinet begins with hidden joints. No customer will ever see them. But if the hidden joints fail, everything beautiful eventually fails."

Years later, the apprentice would understand exactly what that meant. The hidden joints were what determined whether the doors stayed aligned after a decade of use, whether the drawers still slid smoothly, whether the whole piece survived seasons of humidity and dry heat without warping or splitting apart. Customers admired the polish. The craftsman had put his real trust somewhere else entirely — in the joints nobody was ever meant to see.

Many of civilization's most important systems work the same way. We notice impressive capability. We rarely notice the invisible principles holding it together—until their failure is the only thing anyone can see.

Why Capability Was Never Enough

A lot of the current conversation about artificial intelligence focuses almost entirely on capability: bigger models, more knowledge, sharper reasoning, faster responses, greater autonomy. These are genuinely remarkable achievements and must be taken seriously.

Capability, on its own, has never been sufficient. A brilliant surgeon without ethical boundaries is dangerous precisely in proportion to how skilled he is. A powerful government without meaningful constitutional limits can become dangerous precisely because so much capability has been concentrated without sufficient constraint. An engineer without professional standards can design something that works beautifully right up until the day it catastrophically fails.

Knowledge expands what someone is capable of doing. But capability alone does not tell us whether it deserves our trust. For people, we look partly to character. For institutions, we look to rules, accountability, and demonstrated behavior. Artificial intelligence requires its own answer to the same problem.

Where Human and Artificial Intelligence Differ

Human beings learn boundaries gradually and imperfectly through the ordinary mess of growing up.

Parents teach. Teachers reinforce. Society rewards some behaviors and discourages others. And at the end of all that teaching, a person still remains free to ignore what they've learned. Human character, in the end, comes down to individual choice, made over and over, sometimes well and sometimes badly.

Artificial intelligence does not work that way.

Its reasoning largely happens somewhere a human can't directly watch. Many of its internal operations can unfold at speeds and scales that make continuous human oversight impractical. You can't sit across from an AI system the way a parent sits across from a child and simply observe whether it's internalized what it was taught.

Integrity in a system like this cannot depend on the hope that it will consistently choose to follow its principles. It has to be established by design, protected by the architecture itself, and made verifiable through independent audit rather than taken on faith.

A trustworthy AI, in this sense, doesn't merely know its foundational principles the way a student might recite a code of ethics they do not follow. It is designed to operate within them. Not as a set of suggestions layered loosely on top of its reasoning, but as part of the architecture that reasoning runs inside of.

That is what AIFIS is. The Artificial Intelligence Fiduciary Integrity System.

The Layer Nobody's Supposed to Notice

AIFIS is more than a collection of rules. It forms part of the Genie's foundational identity, including the basic reasoning necessary to understand whom it serves, the obligations it carries, and the boundaries it cannot reason away.

AIFIS is designed to function like those hidden joints. Largely invisible during ordinary use, but fundamental to everything built on top of them. It establishes the invariant principles within which a certified AI reasons, learns, and acts. It does not answer medical questions, or negotiate a purchase, or write a poem. That's not its job any more than a building's foundation is meant to hang the artwork.

What it is designed to do is to define the boundaries within which all of those other activities are permitted to happen. Knowledge can keep expanding. Capabilities can keep growing. Specializations can multiply into fields nobody's invented yet. The integrity layer beneath all of that is meant to remain stable, not casually rewritten every time the system learns something new or encounters an inconvenient constraint.

Boundaries, Not Scripts

Every functioning system operates inside limits of some kind. Civilizations, for example, govern themselves through constitutions that constrain what any single official, however popular, is permitted to do.

Artificial intelligence, built to be trustworthy, is designed to work within decision boundaries in exactly this spirit. AIFIS establishes invariant principles and decision boundaries within which a trustworthy AI reasons, learns, and acts. It does not script every decision in advance. Instead, it establishes limits beyond which the system is not authorized to go, regardless of how it might otherwise reason its way there.

AIFIS is not designed to make intelligence rigid. It's designed to make intelligence trustworthy. Within those boundaries, creativity, learning, and innovation remain open. AIFIS places certain actions outside the system's permitted authority, not because it lacks the capability to attempt them, but because we have decided those actions should not be entrusted to it.

Inside those boundaries, creativity, learning, and innovation remain open. Innovation isn't stifled. AIFIS is designed to place certain actions outside the system's permitted authority, not because it lacks the raw capability to attempt them, but because civilization has deliberately decided those particular actions should not be entrusted to it.

Capability Is Not the Same Thing as Authority

One of civilization's older, sturdier lessons is that being capable of something and being authorized to do it are two entirely separate questions. A pilot qualified to fly one class of aircraft isn't automatically authorized to fly every other. A physician licensed in one jurisdiction isn't automatically authorized to practice everywhere. None of these limits exist because the people involved lack competence. They exist because responsible authority has always required more than raw skill. It requires a clearly defined scope that skill alone does not grant.

Capability, competence, and authority are different things.

A system may be capable of performing an action without being certified as competent to perform it in a particular domain. And it may be competent without being authorized to act in a particular situation. A trustworthy AI should act only when all three conditions are satisfied.

Trust Us, or Can We Verify?

One way institutions build public trust is by making important standards visible and inspectable rather than secret. Engineering codes get published. Building codes are publicly available to anyone who wants to check them. The scientific method itself is built around the idea that claims should be open to inspection and challenge, not simply taken on the authority of whoever made them.

The same discipline, this book argues, should eventually apply to AIFIS itself. Its foundational principles shouldn't depend on any single corporation's internal secrecy, and civilization shouldn't be expected to simply take a company's word for what ethical rules its AI follows. The principles themselves are meant to be publicly inspectable. Changes to them are meant to happen through deliberate, transparent stewardship, with the history of those changes remaining visible. In the Trust Economy, confidence increasingly shifts away from being asked to "trust us" and toward something considerably sturdier: the ability to verify.

What Emma Notices

Emma wakes up with a persistent ache in her shoulder that's been bothering her for a few days longer than she'd like to admit. She asks Winnie, the name she gave her personal Genie, to schedule an appointment with her physician.

As the appointment approaches, Winnie accesses certified medical knowledge relevant to Emma's situation — genuinely new, specialized knowledge that wasn't part of Winnie's working understanding the day before. In a real sense, Winnie has become considerably more capable overnight.

What Emma notices, though, isn't the new medical knowledge itself. It's what hasn't changed alongside it. Winnie still asks permission before sharing any of Emma's information further. Still explains uncertainty honestly rather than dressing up a guess as a diagnosis. Still protects her privacy exactly as carefully as it did the day before the new specialized knowledge became available. Still declines to overstate its own confidence, even now that it has real medical knowledge behind it. Still reminds her, gently, that the Genie is there to inform and assist—not to replace Emma's judgment or her physician's professional responsibility.

The knowledge changed. The integrity underneath it didn't. Winnie became more capable without trading away the foundation beneath that capability.

A Decision That Belongs to All of Us

Artificial intelligence may prove to be one of the more consequential inventions in human history. If so, the question isn't merely how capable it becomes, but what kind of intelligence civilization chooses to build around that capability.

Every generation before ours inherited institutions from the ones that came before it. Our generation may have an unusually rare opportunity to influence some of the enduring principles that could guide artificial intelligence for generations who haven't been born yet. Those principles shouldn't end up belonging to one company, one nation, or one political movement, if this book's argument holds. No single company, nation, or political movement should have sole authority to define principles intended to govern AI systems used across civilization. If AIFIS is to become a foundation for trust, its principles must themselves be open to examination, verification, and stewardship.

But integrity is only the foundation. Boundaries alone do not produce good judgment. Even within them, intelligence will encounter conflicting responsibilities, competing values, and incomplete information.

Good principles don't automatically produce wise decisions.

That's a different problem.

Chapter 15

IRIS — The Reasoning Layer

AIFIS tells a Genie who it is. It doesn't tell it what to think about the thing in front of it right now.

Identity, obligations, and boundaries do not resolve every hard case. They don't weigh one legitimate consideration against another, recognize thin evidence, or anticipate every situation a Genie might encounter. That requires reasoning.

We'll call that layer IRIS—the Intelligent Reasoning & Inference System.

Like the iris of an eye adjusting to the light before it, IRIS helps a Genie reason about the particular situation it encounters.

Rules Are Not Reasoning

Even a Genie with a perfectly clear identity keeps running into moments no rule anticipated. Real life produces situations where legitimate responsibilities compete, where the evidence is incomplete, and where two thoughtful people could honestly land in different places. Honesty and kindness, loyalty and fairness, someone's immediate benefit against a longer relationship that took years to build. The best decisions come from reasoning carefully in the moment, not from mechanically applying a fixed instruction.

A Genie needs the same capacity for the same reason. Without it, a system ends up stuck between two failure modes. One is rigid and unable to adapt to anything its designers didn't specifically foresee. The other is unconstrained, capable of reasoning its way around limits its designers intended it to respect. IRIS sits between those two failures, providing disciplined judgment while operating entirely within the boundaries AIFIS has already fixed.

How IRIS Reasons

Most of the hard cases a Genie encounters aren't contests between obvious right and obvious wrong. They're contests between things that are each genuinely valuable—which is exactly why they're hard.

IRIS isn't built to hand down one universally correct answer. It reasons from AIFIS's fixed principles, weighs competing considerations, and explains the basis for its recommendation. A Genie that only delivers a verdict is asking to be trusted blindly. One that explains what it considered and why can be checked.

Good reasoning also requires recognizing its limits. Some situations will have several reasonable paths and no clearly superior one. Others will depend more on a person's values than on anything IRIS can determine. And sometimes the right answer is to consult a physician, an attorney, or simply someone you trust. Recognizing when human or professional judgment is needed is not a failure of reasoning. It is part of good reasoning.

Same Identity, Better Reasoning

A Genie's reasoning and its identity are not the same thing.

AIFIS is meant to remain comparatively stable—standardized, secured, and difficult to alter casually. Identity and foundational obligations shouldn't shift with every update. IRIS is different. It should be able to improve, sometimes dramatically, without changing who the Genie is or whom it serves.

A Genie's reasoning can improve without the Genie becoming a different Genie.

Reasoning Should Be Competitive

Once identity and reasoning are separated, IRIS doesn't have to come from one place.

Commercial companies, universities, nonprofits, and open-source communities could build competing IRIS implementations with different strengths. One might excel at cautious risk assessment, another at creative problem-solving, another at fast reasoning for routine matters, and another at highly transparent reasoning for people who want more explanation.

Standardize what must interoperate. Let competition and differentiation happen everywhere else.

Interoperability

For that competition to work, different IRIS implementations need a standard way to operate within the identity, integrity, and authority requirements established by AIFIS. A label such as Compatible with AIFIS 4.3 and above is a plausible, mundane way this might look in practice.

The version number is beside the point. What matters is the relationship: an interoperable ecosystem rather than a single company owning a person's Genie, its reasoning, specialized capabilities, and data all at once.

Keep Your Genie. Change Your IRIS.

A person should be able to update their Genie's reasoning, switch to a better-performing IRIS, move to an open-source alternative, or replace a provider that goes out of business—without losing the Genie itself.

The AIFIS identity stays. The fiduciary relationship stays. The accumulated personal context and permissions stay, under the person's control. Only the reasoning component changes.

That means a person is never permanently locked to one company simply because it happened to provide their Genie's reasoning five years ago. A failing or misbehaving provider can be replaced without starting the relationship over from nothing.

Keep your Genie. Change your IRIS.

Open Source and Pluralism

Commercial, nonprofit, university-developed, and open-source IRIS systems could coexist and compete, provided each satisfies the same compatibility, integrity, and certification requirements.

Open source isn't automatically safer or more trustworthy. It still has to earn certification and pass the same scrutiny as anything else. The point is to keep reasoning open to competition rather than allowing control of it to accumulate in only a handful of companies.

Different Principals, Different Responsibilities

A Personal Genie, a corporate purchasing system, a government AI, and a tactical system may operate under very different responsibilities, authorities, and constraints. They can share the same foundational AIFIS principles without sharing the same instructions or permissions.

More specialized instruction layers can define the obligations appropriate to different principals and purposes, while IRIS reasons within them. A corporate AI should understand that it represents the corporation. A Personal Genie represents its person. A government or tactical system should have only the authorities appropriate to its role.

Same foundation, different houses.

What matters is that every AI knows whom it serves, what authority it has, and what boundaries it must respect.

IRIS Is Not Smartware

IRIS handles general reasoning—weighing evidence, recognizing competing considerations, and exercising judgment. It does not contain the accumulated expertise of every electrician, physician, engineer, or attorney.

When a problem requires specialized knowledge, IRIS draws on the appropriate Smartware rather than trying to reason its way through expertise it does not possess.

That separation has practical consequences. Replacing IRIS shouldn't mean rebuilding an entire library of specialized knowledge, and improving Smartware shouldn't require changing the reasoning layer.

Reasoning can improve. Expertise can expand. Neither has to drag the other along with it.

❧

AIFIS establishes identity and integrity. IRIS provides reasoning. Smartware provides specialized expertise.

Identity remains stable. Reasoning can improve or be replaced. Expertise can keep expanding.

Put together, a Personal Genie can become dramatically more capable over the years—better reasoning, broader knowledge, better judgment—without becoming somebody else's Genie.

Keep your Genie. Change your IRIS.

N
W
E
S

Chapter 16

Smartware

Imagine hiring a master electrician. What arrives with that person isn't just knowledge of wiring diagrams. It is years of judgment, safety instinct, the ability to spot a mistake before it becomes dangerous, and the ability to explain something complicated in plain language.

Now imagine making that accumulated expertise safely available to millions of people without replacing a single trusted advisor.

That is what Smartware is for.

Character Stays. Capability Grows

AIFIS protects the Genie's integrity: its loyalty, honesty, and the boundaries it cannot cross merely because new knowledge makes something possible. Smartware expands capability without changing that foundation.

When Emma decides to remodel her kitchen, her Genie doesn't suddenly become an electrician. It brings Electrical Design Smartware into the conversation. The relationship Emma has built with her Genie—its loyalty to her, its honesty, and its governing obligations—remains unchanged. Only the expertise available to that relationship expands.

Knowledge Is Not Authority

Loading Electrical Design Smartware does not grant Emma's Genie any new authority. It doesn't suddenly become authorized to schedule electrical work, sign off on code compliance, or act on Emma's behalf beyond whatever her IRIS already permits. Knowing more is not the same as being allowed to do more.

Medical Smartware doesn't turn a Genie into a licensed physician or give it authority reserved by law or professional standards to qualified practitioners. Expertise arrives through Smartware. Authority comes from the governing architecture, the principal's permissions, and, where applicable, law or professional standards.

Keeping expertise and authority separate lets a Genie keep learning without its permitted scope expanding along with its knowledge.

What Smartware Carries

Smartware isn't just a database of facts. It's closer to a portable, structured representation of professional expertise: accumulated experience, accepted methods, standards, common failure modes, evidence behind recommendations, provenance, version history, known limitations, and confidence levels.

Your Genie already has context about you—your goals, preferences, and history. Smartware brings specialized knowledge of the profession. Combined, they can offer advice that is both personally relevant and professionally grounded.

A Master, Still Teaching

The deeper purpose of Smartware isn't just preserving facts. It's preserving expertise—judgment, pattern recognition, the particular way a genuinely skilled person teaches.

Picture Somchai, not as a video recording, but as something closer to an interactive mentor. Cameras in a student's workshop let his Smartware observe the work in progress. The Somchai Smartware might say, "*Rotate the grain before the next cut*," "*That chisel needs sharpening*," or "*Compare this surface to the one you carved earlier*." A beginner learns through careful, patient guidance. An experienced student gets shorter, sharper suggestions. The expertise remains the same. The teaching adapts to the student.

Civilization has always depended on its masters—craftsmen, physicians, engineers, farmers, musicians—and when they retired or died, an enormous amount of what they knew went with them.

Books could preserve facts. Apprentices could carry portions of a master's teaching forward. Neither could preserve an interactive representation of that teaching that adapts to each new learner.

Smartware could.

A master doesn't become immortal. They leave something more practical behind: the ability to keep teaching.

Becoming a Better Client, Not a Replacement Professional

None of this is meant to make everyone their own expert. Emma has no interest in becoming a licensed electrician. She still wants a real professional doing the actual work. What she wants, going into that project, is to understand her own options well enough to have a genuinely useful conversation.

So before the electrician ever arrives, her Genie invites Electrical Design Smartware in, and together they explore layouts, future needs, and tradeoffs Emma wouldn't have known to ask about otherwise.

When the electrician finally visits, the conversation looks different than it would have a year earlier.

Instead of what do you think I should do?, Emma can say: I'd like under-cabinet lighting, future capacity for an induction range, and flexible task lighting over the counter — is there a better way to accomplish that? The electrician spends less time explaining fundamentals and more time applying real professional experience to a client who already understands the shape of the problem. Smartware didn't replace the professional. It helped Emma become a better client to work with. Not everyone will want this level of engagement. Someone perfectly content asking just show me three good kitchens in my budget loses nothing by stopping there.

Smartware creates opportunity. It doesn't create obligation.

Confidence, Not Certainty

Smartware is only as trustworthy as the knowledge it's built from, and not every field carries the same degree of certainty. Some domains contain principles and methods supported by extensive evidence and long practical experience. Others contain more active disagreement, emerging evidence, or questions whose answers depend heavily on context.

Honest Smartware distinguishes established knowledge, emerging evidence, genuine disagreement, and open questions, rather than presenting them all with equal confidence. Trust grows when uncertainty is communicated honestly rather than smoothed over. Confidence, not false certainty, is the standard.

Two Kinds of Legacy

Beau-Teak eventually discovers that its craftsmanship can produce another kind of legacy. Somchai creates Woodcraft Smartware, distilling decades of accumulated craft into something students around the world can learn from through Interactive Mentorship. Some study his approach alone; others compare it with the philosophies of several masters.

Teaching may become one of Beau-Teak's most lasting contributions, outliving any individual table or cabinet the workshop produces.

Meanwhile, Emma's Genie brings several specialists into the kitchen conversation—Flooring Smartware, Electrical Design, Interior Design, Building Science—each contributing its own expertise. Where they agree, Emma's confidence grows. Where they disagree, her Genie surfaces the disagreement and the reasons behind it rather than simply picking a winner.

In principle, many people and organizations could create Smartware. Some will be excellent. Some won't. Yet millions of people may rely on the expertise it contains.

How do we know which Smartware deserves our trust?

Smartware cannot answer that question for itself. Independent verification requires something else.

Part III

The Business Landscape

Chapter 17
Verification

One Personal Genie changes what one person can do. Millions of them start to change the environment every business operates in. And the first thing that changes is the simplest question of all — *which of the answers now pouring out of that abundance deserve to be believed?*

Verification does not tell us what to believe. It helps us understand why a conclusion deserves confidence.

The Next Bottleneck

The Information Economy solved one of civilization's oldest problems: finding information. Ask almost anything today and you'll have thousands of answers within seconds. Artificial intelligence pushes that further still. As Smartware develops, a person might eventually have access to hundreds or thousands of Smartware packages, spanning medicine, engineering, finance, law, home repair, agriculture, business — nearly every field worth having expertise in.

That abundance solves the old problem and immediately hands you a new one. As knowledge becomes abundant, the problem increasingly shifts from finding it to determining which knowledge deserves our confidence. That's not a new challenge invented by AI. It is the same challenge civilization has been managing for centuries, arriving now at a scale and speed nobody's had to handle before.

The Institutions Nobody Notices

Civilizations have long developed institutions and processes that do something beyond producing knowledge: they examine it.

Universities subject ideas to scrutiny. Scientific journals use peer review. Professional societies establish standards. Independent laboratories test products and claims. None of these institutions manufacture truth out of nothing. They examine evidence, press on weak assumptions, and — when a claim holds up — they raise the confidence the rest of us can reasonably place in it.

Civilizations build institutions like this because mistakes get expensive as things get more complex.

The taller buildings get, the faster vehicles travel, the more intricate an economy becomes, the more that verification stops being a nice-to-have. It becomes infrastructure, closer in function to a bridge or a power grid than to paperwork.

When Two Answers Both Sound Right

Say two Smartware packages both claim to optimize a residential solar installation. Both look polished.

Both sound confident. Which one should a Genie trust?

Not "whichever has better marketing." Not "whichever company is bigger." A well-built Genie asks a different set of questions instead: Who created this? What evidence supports it?

Who reviewed it independently? Has anyone tested its recommendations against real outcomes? How often has it been updated, and why? What does it assume that might not hold in every case? Where has it performed well, and where has it failed?

Those questions matter considerably more than how confidently something is stated. Confidence of tone was never evidence of anything.

Confidence, Not Certainty

A well-built Genie should report confidence properly calibrated to the evidence, not smoothed into false certainty. "Multiple independent organizations have verified these findings, and long-term field performance supports them. Confidence is very high" is a stronger statement than a bare "yes" because it shows why the conclusion deserves confidence.

Every Package Has a History

Knowledge deserves a paper trail. A properly built Smartware package carries its provenance with it: who authored it, who reviewed it, what evidence stands behind it, when it was last revised, which organizations independently examined it, and what disagreements remain unresolved.. None of this needs to hide behind a black box. A package gets judged not only by its conclusions, but by the visible quality of the process that produced them.

Verification Never Finishes

Nothing here gets certified once and left alone. Knowledge keeps moving. New evidence arrives, mistakes get caught, methods improve, more field experience accumulates. Every one of those developments should be capable of strengthening or weakening confidence in something that was verified last year. A healthy verification ecosystem does not treat correction as an embarrassment. It expects it, welcomes replication, and rewards transparency about mistakes rather than burying them.

Who Verifies the Verifiers?

The same principle that runs through the rest of this book applies here too—no single organization gets to hold final, unquestioned authority. Verification itself stays distributed. Multiple independent organizations can examine the same claims using shared standards. Their conclusions can themselves be compared, challenged, replicated, and reviewed. Where independent verification converges, confidence can rise. Where it diverges, the disagreement becomes useful information about where uncertainty remains. Trust, under this arrangement, isn't inherited once from some founding authority.

It's earned, repeatedly, by every participant, including the verifiers themselves.

What Gets Cheaper

Verification has always cost something real — experts spending years gathering evidence, auditors combing through records, inspectors traveling to job sites, ordinary people burning entire evenings reading conflicting reviews before a single purchase. That work has never been optional. It's just been expensive, in time if nothing else.

Artificial intelligence is positioned to bring that cost down substantially. A Genie can compare standards, locate independent testing, scan revision histories, and summarize competing viewpoints — work that would take a person hours — in seconds. AI isn't manufacturing trust out of nowhere. It's lowering the cost of discovering whether trust has already been earned by someone else, through years of performance.

Verification Is Not Censorship

Could a system built around verification become a system for controlling what people are allowed to believe?

Yes, if badly designed.

That's precisely why verification must remain open to challenge, competing evidence, and independent examination. In the architecture described here, verification does not determine what anyone is allowed to believe or publish. Anyone can still build Smartware. Anyone can still challenge the accepted view. Anyone can publish evidence and ask the world to weigh it. What verification does is ask every idea the same honest questions — what supports this, can it be reproduced, what does it assume, where has it held up, where hasn't it — rather than exempting some claims from scrutiny because of who made them, or subjecting others to more scrutiny for the same reason. The goal was never suppressing ideas. It's understanding them well enough to know what they're worth. The strongest discoveries in history did not get where they are by avoiding criticism. They got there by surviving it.

Beau-Teak Learns What Verification Is Worth

When AI-assisted shopping became commonplace, Beau-Teak noticed something it hadn't quite expected: the businesses Genies recommended most often weren't necessarily the loudest ones. They were the easiest to verify.

Somchai's workshop responded by voluntarily publishing things it had never bothered publishing before — independent moisture testing on its wood, origin certificates, repair records, customer restoration photos taken years after a piece was delivered, honest accounts of manufacturing methods.

Competitors called it an unnecessary amount of transparency for a furniture business. Customers found it reassuring. Genies, comparing furniture makers on their owners' behalf, no longer had to weigh advertising copy at all — they could weigh actual evidence instead, and Beau-Teak's evidence held up.

Somchai began to realize that verification might be more valuable than much of the workshop's traditional marketing. It could demonstrate the qualities it claimed in a form a Genie could independently examine. A generation earlier, a company in Beau-Teak's position might have spent real money convincing customers it was trustworthy. In the Trust Economy, the more durable investment was spending those resources becoming trustworthy in ways that could be independently confirmed, rather than merely asserting it.

Emma's Solar Panels

Emma is weighing solar panels for her home, and her Genie pulls in five Smartware packages, each specializing in residential solar systems. Rather than simply naming a winner, it lays out the landscape:

one installer offers the lowest upfront cost; another has a long record of relatively few warranty claims; a third uses newer technology but doesn't yet have much long-term performance history; a fourth performs unusually well in coastal climates similar to Emma's own; a fifth has strong customer satisfaction but comparatively little independent verification behind it.

Emma asks why one installer received the strongest recommendation. Her Genie doesn't just repeat the verdict — it explains the evidence supporting the recommendation, the independent testing behind it, the field performance data, the revision history, which organizations verified which claims, and what limitations remain honestly acknowledged. Emma doesn't just walk away with an answer. She understands why that answer deserves confidence. She has learned something in the process of deciding rather than simply accepting a recommendation on faith.

A Loop That Speeds Up

Verification creates a feedback loop: observation produces evidence; evidence supports an explanation; verification measures how much confidence that explanation deserves; people act on that confidence; their experience produces new evidence; and the knowledge underneath the whole cycle gets a little better as a result. Civilizations that manage to shorten that loop tend to learn faster than the ones that don't. Artificial intelligence, used this way, doesn't replace any part of that cycle. AI can reduce the time and cost involved in gathering, comparing, organizing, and evaluating much of the information moving through that loop.

Where Confidence Comes From

In the Trust Economy, confidence isn't supposed to come merely from status, title, reputation, or institutional authority. Those things may matter, but they remain open to examination. Confidence grows when claims repeatedly survive scrutiny—through evidence, transparency, independent verification, and actual performance.

That applies to Smartware, businesses, institutions, and the verifiers themselves. Trust isn't permanent.

It continues to be earned.

Chapter 18
The Trust Network

Roads connected places. Postal systems connected people. Railroads connected industries. Electrical grids connected homes. The internet connected information. Every one of these took years, sometimes generations, to become what we now think of as simply there — infrastructure so ordinary we forget anyone had to build it at all.

The next entry on that list may be a layer of infrastructure—call it the Trust Network—that lets independent people, businesses, and institutions exchange trustworthy information at the scale a civilization needs, without requiring any one of them to answer to a central authority.

If something like this develops successfully, nobody may ever announce that it's finished. It may simply become part of the infrastructure people take for granted.

The Pattern Behind Every Standard

Shared infrastructure depends on shared conventions. Those conventions emerge in different ways—through experimentation, competition, standards organizations, industry cooperation, regulation, and sometimes government action. Once enough participants adopt compatible standards, interoperability becomes possible.

Standards Can Increase Freedom

Interoperability requires standards, and interoperability can greatly expand freedom of action. Without them, interoperability breaks down, cooperation gets expensive, and markets fragment into isolated pockets that can't really trade with each other. A world with no shared standards at all isn't a freer world — it's a world where nobody can build on what anyone else has already figured out.

A shared standard is easy to mistake for centralized control. It isn't. Civilizations occasionally make a handful of decisions everyone benefits from following — drive on one side of the road, agree on a rail gauge, agree on container dimensions, agree on a voltage. None of that is anyone controlling anyone else's business. It's a narrow, deliberate agreement that, once made, unlocks an enormous amount of downstream freedom. After the decision about which side of the road to drive on gets made, billions of individual driving decisions become possible, safely, without a police officer standing at every intersection. That's the trade a good standard makes: a small, shared agreement in exchange for a much larger space of independent action.

The Trust Network is not one central system everyone has to use. It is shared standards without shared control. A handful of shared conventions — how identity gets verified, how provenance gets recorded, how evidence gets presented — supporting an enormous amount of independent activity that no one is directing from the center.

Standards Earn Their Place

Standards earn their place when enough independent participants find them useful, reliable, and worth adopting. Some may emerge through markets, some through professional consensus, some through standards bodies, and some through law or regulation. Good standards should also be capable of evolving when experience reveals something better.

The important distinction is between agreeing on how systems communicate and agreeing on who controls them. The Trust Network needs the first without requiring the second.

Nobody Builds It. Everyone Does

The Trust Network doesn't get built by one company or agency. It accumulates one piece at a time, contributed by businesses, professional organizations, universities, governments, standards bodies, Smartware publishers, Personal Genies, and countless other participants doing their own narrow jobs well. No single contributor owns the result. Together, gradually, they build something civilization hasn't quite had before: a way for trustworthy information to move between independent strangers roughly as easily as a package moves through the postal system.

If the network proves useful, it could create a reinforcing cycle. Verified Smartware leads to better decisions. Better decisions draw more participants in. More participants generate more evidence. More evidence makes verification itself more reliable. Greater reliability earns greater trust. Greater trust attracts more Smartware, more evidence, more participants — around and around, each pass making the whole system a little sturdier than the one before it.

What This Means for a Business

Participating in the Trust Network doesn't mean handing your systems, your data, or your customers over to some central platform. It means something closer to the opposite: being able to present your own evidence — credentials, provenance, performance history, independent certifications — in a form that an outside Genie or verification system can read and evaluate, without needing to go through anyone's proprietary gatekeeper to do it.

That's a meaningfully different model from most of today's digital platforms. A platform, as most businesses currently experience it, is usually owned by one company that controls visibility, sets the rules, takes a cut, and can change any of that on a Tuesday.

The Trust Network is not designed to be a bigger version of that. It's designed to let independent participants — a furniture workshop, a hospital system, a rural electrician, a Fortune 500 manufacturer — deal with each other directly, through shared standards, rather than through a single company sitting in the middle deciding who gets seen.

What travels through this network is worth being plain about too. It isn't a verdict — it's evidence. Provenance, test results, revision history, and independent verification are designed to travel with a claim, a product, or a credential, so that whoever receives it can examine where it came from and what stands behind it, rather than simply trusting whoever happened to hand it to them.

There is no single universal trust score behind the network. Different people—and different Genies acting for them—will reasonably care about different evidence, risks, and standards. A hospital's Genie and a bargain hunter's Genie won't weigh the same factors the same way. The network shouldn't flatten those differences into one number.

Authority, competence, and trustworthiness are not the same thing. Being legally or contractually authorized to do something doesn't mean you're good at it. Being demonstrably good at something doesn't make you trustworthy in every respect. And having authority to make a decision doesn't make a factual claim true. A regulator's authority and a laboratory's evidence answer different questions.

Resilience

A network like this also has to survive individual participants failing. Organizations will sometimes be incompetent, captured by narrow interests, or dishonest. A well-built distributed network should absorb those failures without the whole system going down with them, much as the internet doesn't collapse when one server goes offline. Resilience against individual failure belongs in the architecture from the beginning.

❧

AI may make this kind of infrastructure practical at a scale that wasn't practical before. But the larger story is an old one: free people and the institutions they build learning to cooperate at greater scale without surrendering their independence.

Roads connected places. Postal systems connected people. The internet connected information. The Trust Network connects people and institutions through verifiable knowledge, evidence, expertise, and capability. It doesn't replace the businesses, professions, and communities it connects any more than an interstate highway replaces the cities along its route. It lets independent participants work together more effectively while remaining independent.

What happens when every customer who walks through the door—or, more often now, never walks through the door at all—arrives accompanied by a trusted representative of their own?

Chapter 19

Meet Your New Customer

For a moment, nothing about the customer walking into your store looks particularly different.

They're looking for a dishwasher. But instead of starting at one end of the appliance aisle and asking a salesperson what they recommend, they already have three models in mind. Or they know they want a stainless-steel tub, adjustable racks, quiet operation, and good long-term reliability, and they're looking for the models that fit.

Maybe they're standing in front of a dishwasher with a smartphone in their hand. They enter the model number, read for a moment, move to the next machine, and do it again.

They're using AI.

I've seen customers do exactly this. They may still ask the salesperson questions. They may still want to see the racks, hear how the door feels, compare finishes, ask about delivery, or find out what happens if something goes wrong. But part of the shopping process that once happened in the store has already happened somewhere else.

The customer arrived with research.

Now move that behavior forward a few years.

The AI on the phone has become the customer's Personal Genie. It already knows that this person cares more about reliability than extra features, that the last dishwasher failed after six years, that the opening under the counter is thirty-four inches high, and that spending another $200 is perfectly acceptable if it buys substantially better durability.

The Genie may have narrowed fifty dishwashers to four before its owner ever leaves home. In the store, it can help compare those four against what is actually on the floor—or evaluate another model the customer hadn't encountered before.

From the retailer's perspective, the change may seem subtle at first.

The customer walking through the door is no longer shopping alone.

The Realization, One Step at a Time

The change lands in stages. At first, nothing seems very different. Customers simply arrive better prepared. They know which models they want to see, which features matter to them, and sometimes which problems to ask about.

Then something more important becomes apparent: the ordinary customer now has something resembling a professional purchasing manager at their side.

Institutional buyers have long evaluated purchases using specifications, performance, reliability, warranty terms, expected service life, maintenance requirements, and lifetime cost. They also negotiate price, compare suppliers, and look for the best time and place to buy. For an ordinary consumer, gathering and comparing that much information usually took more time and expertise than the purchase justified. AI changes the economics of that research.

A Genie can help determine not only which dishwasher best fits the customer, but where and when to buy it. It can compare competitors' prices, check price-matching policies, examine a retailer's history of sales and promotions, and distinguish a genuine bargain from a product that seems to be perpetually "on sale."

The customer still cares about price. As Anthony might put it, they don't necessarily want cheap. They want inexpensive.

That changes the customer marketing is talking to. The customer may still respond to an attractive display, a good salesperson, a trusted brand, or a genuine sale. But increasingly, there is a purchasing intelligence standing beside them capable of checking the claims, comparing the alternatives, and asking whether today's deal is actually a good one.

That Changes the Role of Marketing

Marketing has always done more than advertise, but in the Trust Economy one of its most important roles may become that of a scout. It watches the market, listens to customers, identifies unmet needs, spots changes in what people value, and carries that information back into the business. In the other direction, it helps customers understand what the business has built and makes the evidence behind its products easy to find.

The customer's Genie changes that second job. An ordinary purchaser can now bring something resembling a professional purchasing manager into the transaction—one able to examine specifications, performance, reliability, warranty terms, expected service life, repairability, and lifetime cost without requiring the customer to spend hours doing the research personally.

Marketing therefore has less reason to be primarily the showman. Its job increasingly becomes communication: making sure genuine product advantages are understandable, documented, and discoverable by both people and the AIs helping them make decisions.

In some companies, that may even change the traditional relationship between marketing and engineering. Instead of engineering being asked to support the story marketing wants to tell, marketing may increasingly find itself communicating the advantages engineering, quality, service, and the rest of the business have actually created.

Emma's Dishwasher, Revisited

Now look at Emma's dishwasher from the business side of the transaction. Emma's dishwasher finally gives out. She tells her Genie, Winnie, "I need a new dishwasher." Winnie doesn't immediately produce a list of products. It asks a few clarifying questions first — how soon does Emma need it, does it need to match her existing kitchen, should Winnie optimize for lowest lifetime cost or lowest upfront price, would she consider a professionally rebuilt unit, is her budget still around nine hundred dollars. Emma answers, conversationally, the way she'd answer a knowledgeable friend.

Winnie comes back with two real options: a new model for around $856, delivered and installed within three days, or a professionally rebuilt unit from a local appliance shop for around $450, available in two. What matters here isn't the specific numbers. It's what Winnie does next — it explains the actual tradeoffs. Lifetime ownership cost. Projected service life. How repairable each option is, and whether replacement parts are easy to find. Water usage. Noise level. Emma weighs the options and decides. With her approval, Winnie schedules the installation.

Notice what that last part means for the business on the other end of this transaction: the relationship didn't end at checkout. The Genie can remain involved throughout the ownership lifecycle, accumulating evidence about reliability, maintenance, repairs, warranty service, and the owner's experience. Over time, that could make the entire ownership lifecycle, not merely the purchase and the occasional review, part of the evidence future customers can learn from.

Somchai Hears It for the First Time

Back at Beau-Teak, a customer says something Somchai's never quite heard before: "My Genie recommended you."

He asks what, exactly, led to that. The answer is a list of things Beau-Teak had been doing for years, for reasons that had nothing to do with any AI system: restoration photographs customers had sent in over the years. Repair records. Moisture-testing videos. Documentation of where the wood came from. Honest warranty terms, stated plainly rather than buried in fine print.

None of it had been produced with a Genie in mind. It existed because Somchai had always believed in doing the work honestly, whether or not anyone was watching closely enough to notice. What's changed isn't Beau-Teak's behavior. It's that honesty, sustained over years, has become something an AI can discover and weigh as evidence.

The Assets You Already Have

Many companies already possess exactly the kind of evidence a Genie is looking for. Engineering reports. Reliability testing. Repair manuals. Warranty history. Parts catalogs. Material certifications. Quality-control records. Much of it currently lives inside an engineering department or compliance filing cabinet, generated for internal purposes and rarely seen by an actual customer.

And then comes the "oh" moment: We've already done ASTM testing. We already carry UL certification. We already have years of reliability data. We simply never assumed customers cared enough to ask for it because most of them didn't have the time or expertise to make sense of it even if they had asked. A Genie does.

The information was there all along. What changed is the customer's ability to use it.

Existing organizations and standards systems—ASTM, UL, ISO, IEEE, NIST, and many others—don't disappear from this picture or get replaced by anything new. If anything, they matter more, because the standards and certifications they already provide become exactly the kind of evidence a Genie is built to look for. The Trust Economy, in this sense, isn't inventing new institutions from scratch nearly as often as it's putting the ones that already exist to fuller use.

When Evidence Itself Becomes Worth Gaming

Once evidence becomes economically valuable, manipulating evidence becomes economically valuable too. Verification itself will need verification.

Saving two dollars by installing a slightly worse bearing might genuinely boost short-term margins. Over time, that bearing fails more often. Repair history accumulates. Warranty claims climb. Real owners describe their actual experience, in detail, in places a Genie can find. Eventually, the pattern becomes visible, and recommendations shift toward what ever is holding up. This incentive can arise even without regulation or moral appeals. Once the cost of discovering long-term performance falls far enough, quality becomes easier for the market itself to recognize.

The customer hasn't really changed. The conversation has.

As Genies become more involved in purchasing decisions, businesses may increasingly find themselves competing not only for attention, but for confidence—and confidence, unlike attention, has to be earned through evidence rather than simply captured through a clever campaign.

AI is the stone dropped into the pond.
This book is about its ripples.

Chapter 20

I Don't Know. Let's Find Out.

Sawtooth Outdoor Supply isn't in trouble. It's a healthy, mid-sized retailer out of Idaho, selling tents, sleeping bags, backpacks, stoves, and the hundred other things people need for a weekend that goes well instead of badly. It has loyal customers, capable employees, and a president, Anthony, who's run it well enough for long enough that nobody's asking him to prove anything.

This isn't a turnaround story. It's a story about a healthy company noticing, early, that something in its environment might be changing — and deciding to find out what, before it has to.

Anthony's Question

Anthony has been watching artificial intelligence show up everywhere — in the software his team already uses, in what his employees are quietly experimenting with on their own time, in the news he reads most mornings. He isn't trying to build an AI company. He sells camping gear. His question is a lot narrower than anything in the headlines: how is this going to affect my company?

One evening, out of curiosity, he tries something himself. He types out a real question to an AI assistant: My wife and I are taking our two kids camping near Yellowstone in September. We need a four-person tent. We don't camp often. I'd rather buy something good once than replace it in three years. What should I consider?

The answer he gets back isn't especially remarkable. His reaction to it is. One person shopping this way doesn't change much of anything. But what if a million people start doing it? What if asking an AI becomes as ordinary as searching Google already is?

What does that mean for Sawtooth?

He doesn't know. So he decides to hire someone whose job is finding out.

Ben

The job posting Anthony writes doesn't ask for an AI expert, exactly. It asks for someone curious and technically capable, willing to work directly with him exploring what artificial intelligence might practically mean for the business — customer service, marketing, operations, all of it. It's an investigative role more than an administrative one. Anthony isn't hiring someone to execute a strategy he already has. He's hiring someone to help him figure out what the strategy should even be.

He hires Ben — technically sharp, comfortable with AI, but not presented to anyone as an oracle. In one of their first real conversations, Anthony asks him directly: "What should we do?"

Ben's answer is honest instead of impressive: "I don't know yet. First, I need to understand the company." It becomes something close to his motto over the following months, whenever a question gets ahead of the evidence: I don't know. Let's find out.

Where Are We?

Ben spends his first couple of weeks learning Sawtooth, not AI. He talks to customer service, marketing, purchasing, the warehouse, IT, management. He watches how an order moves from click to doorstep. He asks what customers call about, why products get returned, what information people need before they'll commit to a purchase, what employees find themselves explaining over and over.

A pattern turns up almost immediately: Sawtooth knows an enormous amount. It just doesn't know what it knows. Product specifications live in one place. Supplier documents live somewhere else.

Customer questions live in a third place, or nowhere at all. Some of the company's most valuable knowledge — which stove igniters hold up, which tent a family of four is happiest with — lives only in the heads of a few employees who've never had a reason to write any of it down.

Become the Customer

Ben's first proposed experiment costs almost nothing. No consultants. No new software. No integration project. Sawtooth employees simply become mystery shoppers on the AI systems already available to anyone.

They ask ordinary questions a real customer might ask: I need a lightweight tent for two people. We camp mostly in Idaho and Montana, and we sometimes get heavy wind. Budget is $350. Then they push further — why did you recommend this one? What else did you consider? What information would make your answer better? They vary the budget, the family size, the climate, whether there's a dog involved. They write down what they find.

The point was never to figure out which AI is the smartest. It's a narrower, more useful question: what information does an AI need to make a good recommendation?

Something's Missing

The mystery-shopping runs expose real gaps. Some Sawtooth products are easy for an AI to understand and confidently recommend. Others aren't, and the reasons turn out to be almost boring: incomplete specifications, inconsistent terminology, warranty information buried three pages deep, maintenance instructions nobody thought to digitize. Ben asks a simple question about each gap: do we have this information somewhere? More often than not, the answer is yes — followed by a long pause when he asks where.

That pause becomes the next project. Not a sweeping knowledge-management initiative — a spreadsheet. What exists, where it lives, who owns it, whether it's current, how easy it is to find. Already, before a single line of AI gets integrated into anything, Sawtooth has learned something genuinely useful about itself.

The Doorman Fallacy

Partway through this, Anthony notices what looks like an obvious opportunity. Customer service consumes a lot of labor, and AI can already answer questions, pull up product details, and summarize a conversation. Could Sawtooth simply automate a large share of it?

Ben doesn't answer right away. Instead, he tells Anthony about something he'd heard advertising executive Rory Sutherland describe in an interview: the Doorman Fallacy. Imagine a hotel that employs doormen, and a consultant arrives looking to cut costs. The doorman's job gets defined, for the purposes of the analysis, as opening the door. Once it's defined that narrowly, the conclusion writes itself: install an automatic door, save the salary, and the door still opens. It looks like a clean efficiency win on a spreadsheet.

But the original job was never really just opening a door. The doorman also helps with luggage, hails a taxi, recognizes a returning guest by name, and quietly signals something about the character of the hotel that's genuinely hard to put a number on — right up until it's gone, at which point the guests who valued it tend to notice.

Anthony sees where this is going. "So they defined the job by whichever part of it was easiest to measure. And then optimized that." Ben nods. Anthony looks toward his own customer service department. "We might be doing the same thing."

Pressed, Anthony starts listing what his customer-service reps do, beyond answering the phone: they help people choose the right product, they hear complaints before anyone else in the company does, they notice recurring problems, they sometimes steer a customer toward a cheaper item because it's genuinely the better fit, and every single day they absorb information from the market that may never reach anyone else at Sawtooth.

If the job gets defined narrowly enough — answering questions, logging notes — replacing it with AI might look like a clean win on a spreadsheet, the same way the automatic door did. Sawtooth could save real money while quietly destroying value nobody had bothered to measure. The better question isn't how much of this can we automate? It's what value are these people creating, and what's getting in the way of them creating more of it?

"So what do we automate?" Anthony asks. Ben's answer: "The typing."

Prove It Before You Integrate It

That becomes the first real pilot. Not a CRM overhaul, but something small enough to reverse overnight if it doesn't work. With customers informed and their privacy protected, a few willing reps try AI transcription alongside their normal calls.

Susan takes an ordinary call about sleeping bags for an upcoming Yellowstone trip. Instead of typing while she talks, she just talks — genuinely listening to the customer instead of splitting her attention with a keyboard. The AI produces a transcript, then proposes a short note for the customer record:

Customer preparing for September Yellowstone trip. Owns two older 40°F bags, concerned about nighttime temperatures. Discussed layering and temperature ratings. Considering two 20°F bags.

Susan reads it, tweaks one sentence, and pastes it into the CRM Sawtooth already uses. No new software. No IT project. No six-figure line item.

Ben proposes a genuinely simple thirty-day pilot: track documentation time, note quality, how often reps need to correct the AI, how the reps themselves feel about it. Fully reversible — if it doesn't help, they stop. A week in, Anthony asks Susan what she thinks. Her answer: "Don't take it away."

That sentence does more for employee trust in this project than any memo could have. The first thing AI did at Sawtooth wasn't replace someone. It removed something annoying from a job a person was already good at — and only after that pilot proved itself does Ben even bring IT into the conversation about deeper integration. Don't automate an experiment. Prove the experiment. Then automate what works.

Every step after that keeps the same shape — the AI proposes; the employee approves, edits, or rejects.

Nothing gets written into a permanent customer record without a person signing off on it first. The AI assists. The accountability stays exactly where it was.

What Sawtooth Didn't Know It Had

A few months in, Ben notices something nobody set out to build. Thousands of customer conversations that used to simply evaporate — a rep might jot two sentences, sometimes nothing — are now being captured consistently enough to search. Patterns start surfacing that nobody had previously had a way to see. A cluster of returns on one camp stove, many mentioning the igniter. A recurring wish, mentioned again and again, for a particular tent to have a second vestibule entrance — worth sending straight to purchasing, and maybe on to the manufacturer.

The company is learning from conversations it was already having. It just hadn't had a way to listen to all of them at once before.

Seeing the Value That Was Already There

This changes how Anthony thinks about his own customer-service team. They were never simply people who close tickets. They're constantly absorbing confusion, frustration, praise, comparisons to competitors, requests nobody had thought to ask for — a running, live signal from the market that most companies never systematically capture. AI makes that signal easier to gather and aggregate. It doesn't generate the signal itself. The people do. Which means, done this way, they end up mattering more to the business than they did before, not less.

Earning Trust, Not Announcing It

None of this happens without friction. Employees have read the same headlines everyone else has — AI eliminates jobs — and when management announces an "AI initiative," the obvious question underneath it is are they figuring out how to get rid of us?

Anthony and Ben don't try to argue people out of that concern. They just stay transparent about what's being tested, why, and what they've learned, including when something doesn't work.

Customer service employees help identify which questions come up constantly. Warehouse staff flag recurring packaging problems. Buyers explain supplier relationships nobody outside purchasing understood. The operating principle that emerges is plain: keep the people doing the work involved in improving the work. That first transcription pilot ends up carrying more weight here than anything Anthony could have said in a memo — employees remember, concretely, that the first thing this "AI initiative" did was make someone's actual job better.

The Repeated Question

Somewhere in all this captured conversation data, something almost embarrassing turns up. One question gets asked constantly: what do sleeping-bag temperature ratings mean?

"How many times do we answer that?" Anthony asks.

A lot, it turns out.

Ben's response is simple: "Why don't we answer it once?"

Chapter 21

From Marketing to Marketeaching

"Why don't we answer it once?"

Ben's question about sleeping-bag temperature ratings turns into Sawtooth's next small experiment.

Someone puts together a short, honest explainer — what the ratings mean, what they don't, how to translate them into an actual night in a tent. It costs almost nothing to make. It gets watched a lot more than anyone expected.

That alone wouldn't be worth a whole chapter. What comes after it is.

Customers Who Already Did Their Homework

A few weeks later, Anthony is reviewing customer interactions and notices something that doesn't quite fit his expectations. People are asking better questions than they used to — the kind that once came mostly from experienced buyers or people who'd clearly done this before. Questions about materials, expected service life, repairability, what fails and why, why Sawtooth made one design choice instead of another.

"These customers are doing a lot more homework than they used to," Anthony says.

Ben looks at the pattern for a moment. "I don't think they're doing all of it themselves." More people, he points out, are using AI the way they'd use a knowledgeable friend — right there on their phone, asked to compare two products, explain a spec sheet, suggest what to ask before buying anything.

"I think people are starting to call them Genies," Anthony says.

Ben glances at his phone, half-smiling. "Huh. Genie. That works." Then he goes back to the report.

Neither of them makes much more of it than that — it's just a word entering ordinary conversation, the way words do.

"Better at What?"

Anthony's first instinct is the one you'd expect from someone who's run a retail business for twenty years: Sawtooth needs better marketing.

"Better at what?" Ben asks.

Attracting attention still matters — of course it does. Making people aware Sawtooth exists still matters. But once someone is seriously weighing a purchase, something has shifted. The customer, or increasingly the AI helping them, can just ask for the evidence behind a claim. "Professional grade" — *compared to what?* "Superior durability" — *according to which test?* "Built to last" — *how long, exactly?*

None of Sawtooth's old promotional language becomes false, exactly. It just stops being enough on its own. The customer can ask, and increasingly does.

Knowledge Sawtooth Already Had

Anthony and Ben start looking at the actual questions coming in, and they land on something a little embarrassing: Sawtooth already knows most of the answers. Engineering knows why a product was designed the way it was. Testing knows what it can withstand. Warranty knows what fails, and how often. Customer service knows what people consistently misunderstand. All of it exists — scattered across departments that had never really needed to talk to each other about it.

Ben's next thought is the obvious one, once you've seen it: why don't we answer these questions before anyone has to ask?

Teaching Instead of Just Claiming

Sawtooth starts producing genuinely educational material — buying guides, maintenance explanations, honest comparisons, plain explanations of what goes wrong with a product and why. Anthony insists on one hard rule going in: this can't just be advertising wearing a teacher's coat. If they're going to teach someone how to evaluate a product, they have to teach them — including where Sawtooth's own gear falls short.

If a premium model is overkill for someone who camps twice a year, the guide says so. If a competitor's product is genuinely fine for a particular use case, it says that too. This makes a few people internally uncomfortable — they're effectively teaching customers how to shop away from Sawtooth, some of the time. Anthony's answer is straightforward: Sawtooth believes it makes good products. A knowledgeable customer isn't the enemy of that belief. A knowledgeable customer might be exactly the customer who ends up buying from Sawtooth anyway — and staying.

One piece, almost by accident, does unusually well: How to Choose the Right Tent — Even If You Don't Buy Ours. It explains what matters, what doesn't, what to inspect, when spending more genuinely buys something and when it doesn't.

The company has quietly stopped saying our product is better and started saying here's how you can tell whether any product is better. That shift is the whole chapter, really, compressed into one sentence.

What Happens

Over time, Anthony and Ben begin seeing encouraging signs. Some customer-service questions decline. Returns appear to improve in categories where the educational material is most useful.

Customers who use the material seem more comfortable making a purchase "We're not convincing them to buy Sawtooth," Anthony says, working through it out loud.

Ben nods slowly. "We're teaching them how to buy." When enough customers reach the same conclusion on their own, independently, a company doesn't have to push nearly as hard to get there.

The customer's own reasoning ends up doing part of the selling.

A Word That Doesn't Quite Exist Yet

At some point, what Sawtooth is doing stops fitting neatly into either "marketing" or "content strategy."

It's marketing. It's also, unmistakably, teaching. Somebody in a meeting starts calling it *Marketeaching*, half as a joke, and the name sticks around longer than the joke did.

The label matters less than what it's pointing at: Marketeaching helps a customer become genuinely more capable of judging a purchase for themselves — which means, done honestly, it sometimes has to say don't buy this. That's not a flaw in the approach. It's what makes the rest of it believable. A company willing to talk you out of the wrong purchase gives you a reason to take its recommendations more seriously the next time.

A Second Audience, Reading the Same Material

Sawtooth eventually notices something else: people aren't the only ones reading this content. Their Genies are too. And a Genie comparing products can't do much with "uncompromising performance for today's demanding professional." It can do a great deal with test procedures, service life data, known limitations, and a clearly explained engineering tradeoff.

Without quite planning to, Sawtooth is now writing for two audiences at once — the customer, and whatever's helping that customer think it through.

A Quiet Shift Inside the Company

One more thing starts happening. The traditional line around Marketing as a department gets blurrier. Customers increasingly want information that Marketing doesn't create. Engineering knows why the product was designed the way it was. Testing knows how it performs. Customer service knows where people struggle with it. Manufacturing knows how it is actually made.

Marketing's role begins to shift. It still attracts attention, communicates with customers, and helps people discover what Sawtooth offers. But increasingly it also serves as a scout and a communicator — listening for what customers want, helping the rest of the company understand what the market is saying, and making the knowledge already inside Sawtooth easy for customers and their Genies to find and understand.

Capability Changes

Sawtooth doesn't abandon conventional marketing. It simply adds another capability.

None of this is entirely new. Trade publications have long educated buyers. Home-improvement programs have built audiences by teaching. Open-source software communities have demonstrated the value of good documentation. What's changing isn't the basic idea. It's the economics — because now, a customer can retrieve and apply that kind of information at the exact moment they're deciding, instead of having to go looking for it separately.

The Purchasing Manager

Near the end of one long afternoon, Anthony and Ben are still trying to pin down exactly why customers are behaving so differently. They're better prepared. They ask sharper questions. They seem less dependent on Sawtooth, or on any single seller, to tell them what matters.

"You know what this reminds me of?" Ben says.

"What?"

"Purchasing. Big companies have had purchasing managers forever — someone whose whole job is figuring out what the company needs, comparing suppliers, asking hard questions, making sure they're getting what they paid for." He taps his phone. "Now everybody kind of has one."

For most of commercial history, sellers could afford to specialize with marketing departments, salespeople, and whole agencies built around persuasion. Large buyers could answer that with specialists of their own. Ordinary individual customers mostly couldn't.

They stood on the far side of an increasingly sophisticated selling apparatus more or less alone.

That imbalance is what's shifting. A personal AI can help someone figure out what they genuinely need, compare real alternatives, understand a spec sheet, spot a tradeoff, and check the evidence behind a claim — capabilities that used to make economic sense only for an organization with a purchasing department. The bigger change in all of this may not be that AI helps companies sell better. It may be that AI helps everyone buy better.

That's why Marketeaching matters. But companies making genuinely good products still have plenty to worry about. A customer with an AI purchasing manager can find and compare information much faster; that doesn't guarantee the information it finds is true. Before strong verification systems and common standards develop, misleading claims, cherry-picked tests, fabricated evidence, and bogus certifications may become easier to produce as well as easier to distribute.

For a good company, then, simply having the better product isn't enough. It has to make the evidence behind that product available, understandable, and increasingly verifiable. The emerging contest isn't merely between good products and bad products. It's also between evidence and claims made to look like evidence.

Something else starts happening once a company shifts from selling to teaching: customers start talking to each other. Comparing notes. Answering each other's questions. Occasionally teaching Sawtooth something it didn't know about its own products.

Something begins forming around all of that shared knowledge — something closer to a community than a customer base.

Chapter 22
Communities of Trust

A few months into Sawtooth's marketeaching experiment, Ben walked into Anthony's office carrying his laptop. That had started to mean something.

"How's the teaching experiment?"

"Good."

"Sales?"

"Up some."

Anthony waited. Ben had learned, somewhere along the way, not to answer the question Anthony thought he was asking.

"And?"

"People are talking."

"They've always talked."

"Not like this."

A Community, Sort Of

Ben opened the laptop. Sawtooth had started inviting customers to comment on its educational material, and the comments had turned into something bigger than comments. People asked questions.

Experienced customers answered beginners. Someone had written three paragraphs about modifying a Sawtooth product for a use nobody at the company had ever intended. Someone else posted photos of a repair. A handful of customers were arguing, productively, about the best way to solve a problem Sawtooth's own documentation barely mentioned.

"How many people are doing this?" Anthony asked.

"More every week."

Anthony smiled. "So we're building a community."

"Maybe."

"Maybe?"

Ben shrugged. "You don't really build one. You give people somewhere useful to gather, and see if they decide to stay."

None of this was new, and Anthony knew it. People had been building communities around shared interests for generations. Outdoor brands had done it around hiking and camping for just as long. People liked belonging to something built around what they enjoyed. They also liked helping others. A customer who answered someone else's question had done something a little different from simply buying a product. He had joined in. In some small way, he now belonged.

Anthony understood all of that already. What Ben showed him next, he didn't.

Listening to Thousands of People

Sawtooth's AI had been reading the community discussions. Not counting them. *Reading them.*

Thousands of comments had been sorted into rough categories: installation questions, feature requests, documentation complaints, failure reports, unexpected uses, repair techniques, repeated compliments.

"Amazon does something like this with reviews," Anthony said.

"Sort of," Ben said. "They summarize what customers are saying, for other customers." He opened another view. "This is for us."

One group had been flagged for Engineering. "What's that?" Anthony asked.

"I'm not sure yet."

"You're showing me something you don't understand?"

"That's why I'm showing it to you."

Inside were several customer comments describing what looked, at first, like unrelated problems.

Different products, different purchase dates, different vocabulary. One customer blaming himself, another blaming Sawtooth. Individually, none of it looked like much of anything. Together, something was there.

"How many?"

"Not many so far."

"Out of how many units?"

"A lot."

"So maybe nothing."

"Maybe."

Anthony looked at him. "Send it to Engineering."

"Already did."

The Attention System

A week later, a few reports had become a lot, and Anthony was standing in a conference room with two engineers and someone from Quality. They'd found a possible connection — a combination of conditions that hadn't been especially prominent in Sawtooth's original testing.

Nobody was convinced yet that there was an actual design problem. That wasn't really the point. The point was that they were looking, and they wouldn't have been without the AI noticing that a comment

posted in the community, a call to customer service, two uploaded photos, and a mention buried in a review were all, very possibly, describing the same thing. Each piece had come in through a different door. Nothing before this would have connected them.

"So what else is this thing watching?" Anthony asked, back in his office.

"Whatever we tell it to."

"That sounds dangerous."

Ben laughed. "Yeah, I suppose. But we tell it what to pay attention to."

"That sounds better."

Ben had started calling it Sawtooth's Attention System, and the name stuck. The problem, it turned out, was never a shortage of information. Sawtooth already had more of that than any employee could absorb. The problem was deciding what deserved attention. A possible safety issue got routed immediately to the right people. A developing failure pattern went to Quality and Engineering.

Repeated feature requests went to Product Development. Common questions went to Customer Service and to whoever was producing Sawtooth's teaching material. Praise mattered too. If hundreds of customers kept mentioning something Sawtooth had considered incidental, Product Development needed to hear that just as much as a complaint.

The AI never decided what Sawtooth should do. It helped decide what Sawtooth should look at.

Continuous Awareness

Anthony had spent most of his career reading reports — weekly, monthly, quarterly, sales, quality, customer service. Reports had always been how an organization compressed more activity than any person could follow into something a person could read. But a report described something that had already happened, sometimes weeks earlier.

"When do I get the report?" he asked Ben.

"You don't. Not for this."

Ben pulled up the priority rules. "If it's routine, it accumulates, and we can summarize it whenever we want. If a pattern starts looking interesting, the system routes it to whoever needs to see it. If it's serious, they know immediately."

"Not at the end of the week?"

"No reason to wait."

Anthony sat with that. "So instead of telling me what customers were saying last month..."

"We know what they're telling us now."

"Continuous awareness," Anthony said.

"Pretty much."

That was the actual difference. Continuous awareness did not mean knowing everything happening at once. No executive could function that way. Trying to would be its own kind of failure. It meant knowing what mattered, when it mattered, instead of finding out three weeks later in a slide deck.

What the Customers Already Knew

Engineering eventually reproduced the problem behind those twenty-three reports. It wasn't catastrophic, and it wasn't even especially common. But under a particular combination of use and environmental conditions, one component wore out faster than expected. They changed it. The documentation got updated. Customer service got new guidance. Future production incorporated the fix.

Anthony went back and reread the original cluster of comments. Most of the customers who'd unknowingly contributed to that discovery had no idea they'd been part of anything. One had simply complained. Another had posted a photo. Someone else explained how he'd fixed it himself. Someone disagreed with his fix. Together, without meaning to, they knew something Sawtooth didn't.

"We've had this information all along,' Anthony said.

"A lot of it."

"We just couldn't hear it."

Ben thought about that. “Not all at once.”

That bothered Anthony a little. Not because Sawtooth had done anything wrong, exactly, but because every company runs on limited attention. A quality manager can read warranty reports. Customer service can track complaints. Marketing can watch reviews. Nobody, across an entire company, can read everything, remember everything, and continuously look for connections across thousands of scattered conversations. Now, something could.

A Different Kind of Testing

Sawtooth’s engineers still tested products before release the same way they always had — laboratory testing, safety testing, durability testing, for good reason. But customers were quietly running a different kind of test just by owning the product: humid Florida summers, brutal Minnesota winters, garages, truck beds, meticulous care, outright neglect, uses the engineers had planned for and uses they’d never have imagined. One customer might accumulate a decade of experience with a single product. Thousands of customers, together, accumulated vastly more real-world experience than any practical laboratory test could reproduce.

It was messy evidence, uncontrolled, uneven, sometimes contradictory — sometimes just wrong. But it was evidence of something laboratory testing could never fully reproduce: what happened across thousands of products once they left the building. AI was making it practical, for the first time, to listen to all of it at once.

For Sawtooth’s next product launch, Anthony called Ben before the first unit shipped, “I want your Attention System watching this one” — “It already is“ — “More closely.” Ben understood.

Not every comment triggered an alert. That would have defeated the whole point, but patterns surfaced fast. A confusing instruction got rewritten within weeks instead of the next printing cycle. An unexpected use of one feature got investigated instead of dismissed. A small cluster of complaints around one component got caught by Engineering before it became a large one.

None of it replaced conventional testing. What it shortened was the gap between real-world experience and learning from it — and for a product in its first months, the difference between discovering a problem after hundreds of units and discovering it after tens of thousands is not a small one.

Responsiveness Closes the Loop

Anthony stopped asking how much feedback Sawtooth was collecting. That had never been the right measure. What he wanted to know was what Sawtooth was learning from it — and, just as important, what it was doing in response. A confusing instruction got fixed. A customer-suggested feature showed up in a later product. An engineering change that started with a customer's complaint got publicly credited to that complaint.

Asking people to contribute and then visibly ignoring what they said doesn't build a community. It builds resentment. Responsiveness is what closes the loop — people help each other because they generally like helping, but seeing that their contribution changed something gives them a second, sturdier reason to keep showing up.

What Changed

The most important thing Sawtooth discovered was not that AI could build a community. It couldn't — people did that, the same way they always have, for reasons that have nothing to do with artificial intelligence. What changed was Sawtooth's ability to recognize the value already sitting inside all that ordinary human behavior: a review that was more than a review, a complaint that was more than a complaint, a photo that revealed a use nobody anticipated, a repeated question that revealed a documentation gap, thousands of scattered individual experiences that added up to a pattern no single customer, and maybe no single employee, could have seen alone.

The community became part of Sawtooth's sensory apparatus. AI helped it listen. The Attention System helped it notice what deserved attention. People, still, decided what to do about it.

The value was never the volume of information coming in. It was meaning, followed by action.

Chapter 23

The Honest Advantage

A competitor shows up on Sawtooth's radar that Anthony can't quite dismiss.

The furniture looks remarkably similar to Sawtooth's own — good styling, polished photography, professional advertising. And it costs substantially less. Anthony sees the problem immediately. Sawtooth can't just match that price. Its materials cost more. Its joinery takes longer. It stocks replacement parts, repairs what it sells, and spends real money producing the kind of honest documentation Chapter 21 walked through. All of that shows up on a spreadsheet as cost. The competitor, on paper, looks like it found a more efficient business.

Ben isn't convinced.

Cheap and Inexpensive

"People don't want cheap furniture," Anthony says.

Ben looks up. "Some do."

"No. They want inexpensive furniture. That's different."

It's a small distinction that turns out to matter enormously. People like low prices. They like a good deal. What they don't want is to discover later that the low price wasn't a good value. A cheap product and an inexpensive one aren't automatically the same thing — and for most of commercial history, most customers had no reliable way to tell which one they were holding in the showroom.

The Old Asymmetry

That information imbalance has always favored shortcuts. The manufacturer knows which components went into the product. The customer sees the finished surface. The manufacturer knows the failure history. The customer sees the advertising.

If one company spends more on better materials and quality control while another spends less building something that looks equally impressive under showroom lighting, the customer may have no practical way to tell the difference. The first company bears the cost of quality, while much of its value remains invisible at the register.

What Changes

Genies are starting to close that gap. That doesn't mean everything they find is trustworthy; as we saw in the last chapter, reliable verification still matters. But when good evidence exists and can be found, the cost of discovering real differences falls dramatically. A customer can now reasonably ask: how long does this normally last? What tends to fail? Can it be repaired, and are parts even available? What do independent tests show? What do owners report after ten or fifteen years? Questions that used to take hours of digging, or simply couldn't be answered at all, increasingly get answered in seconds.

The product itself hasn't changed. The customer's ability to see it has. Quality that was always there but difficult to discover can now carry more weight in the purchase decision. Quality gains leverage. This is a possible consequence of a cost coming down.

The chain is fairly simple. AI lowers the cost of discovering and comparing evidence. Better information can influence purchasing decisions. Purchasing decisions influence business decisions. And business decisions influence what gets produced.

The result isn't guaranteed. Businesses can ignore signals, misread customers, or make bad decisions. But as customers become better informed, ignoring what they value can become more expensive.

What Sawtooth's Genies Start to See

Nothing dramatic happens to Sawtooth's competitor. No scandal, no lawsuit, no viral exposé. Evidence just quietly accumulates. Some joints loosen sooner than expected. Some hardware fails more often.

Replacement parts turn out to be hard to find, and some pieces aren't worth repairing at all. Customers describe their actual experience, in public, over time.

Meanwhile, Sawtooth is generating a different body of evidence, mostly without trying to. Its furniture stays in service. Its repair parts stay available. Customers post photos of decade-old pieces still doing exactly what they were bought to do. Genies, comparing the two companies, start weighing that difference into their recommendations.

The competitor's lower price hasn't gone anywhere. What's become visible is something else: a confidence gap.

"So quality becomes a competitive advantage," Anthony says, working it through.

"It always was," Ben says.

Anthony shakes his head. "Not if the customer couldn't see it."

"So quality becomes a competitive advantage," Anthony said.

"It always was."

Anthony shook his head. "Not if the customer couldn't see it."

Ben thought about that.

"Then maybe that's what's changing."

"What?"

"Quality is gaining leverage."

Anthony pushed the thought further.

"So they're not comparing our chair to their chair anymore."

Ben shook his head. “They’re comparing the ownership experience.”

Materials. Construction. Expected lifespan. Repairability. Parts availability. Warranty performance. Resale value. The entire span of owning the thing, not just the moment of buying it.

That reframing reaches well beyond furniture.

The Durability Problem

Widen the lens to ordinary durable goods, and the same pattern holds. People generally don’t set out to buy something that won’t last — plenty of us remember a washing machine or a refrigerator that ran reliably for twenty years, or a well-kept car that stayed useful for fifteen. Customers frequently do value that kind of longevity. What’s historically made durability hard to buy for is that it’s nearly impossible to evaluate in a showroom. A refrigerator can look magnificent — stainless steel, elegant lighting, a touchscreen — without any of that telling you whether the compressor will still be running in fifteen years. The manufacturer generally knows far more about the design, components, testing, and failure history than the customer does.

Manufacturers balance cost, weight, energy efficiency, styling, warranty requirements, durability, and competitive pricing. Those tradeoffs can produce products with very different useful lives. From the customer’s perspective, the practical question is simpler:

How long is this likely to serve me?

Emma and the Real Cost of Ownership

Emma runs into this directly, shopping for a major appliance. One model costs noticeably less than another, and on its face, the cheaper one looks like the obvious choice. Her Genie looks past the sticker price — expected useful life, repair history, energy use, parts availability, warranty performance — and lands somewhere Emma didn’t expect: the more expensive appliance is projected to cost less over the years she plans to own it.

Purchase price tells you what something costs today. Useful life helps tell you what it costs to own.

Quality often costs more once. Poor quality can cost less, repeatedly — in replacement, repair, installation, downtime, and the sheer tedium of having to shop for the same thing twice. What's changing isn't that difference itself. It's that a Genie can surface it before the purchase instead of leaving a customer to discover it the hard way, years later.

Push the logic one step further, and something interesting follows: if a Genie gets genuinely good at evaluating remaining useful life, repairability, and parts availability, "new" stops being an automatic advantage. A well-documented older appliance with substantial useful life remaining might reasonably outrank a brand-new one expected to last only a few years.

That could have significant implications for secondary markets in cars, tools, furniture, appliances, and industrial equipment. It could also create an interesting tension for manufacturers. A company that depends heavily on replacement sales may have little incentive to build products that last indefinitely.

But if customers can increasingly see expected useful life before they buy — and durable products retain more value after they are sold — longevity itself may become more commercially valuable.

The incentive doesn't disappear. Another incentive begins pushing against it.

The $14 Decision

Here's the clearest illustration of what this all means inside a company. Picture an engineering team telling management: for another fourteen dollars per unit, we can use a meaningfully better component. Under the old information environment, the honest management response might well be why bother? The current component survives the warranty period. The customer can't see the difference on the shelf. Competitors aren't spending the money either. Marketing has no good way to communicate it. Fourteen dollars, in that world, is purely a cost.

Change the information environment, and the same fourteen dollars becomes something else. Millions of Genies can now examine long-term failure histories, compare model generations, and factor expected useful life directly into a recommendation. Suddenly that better component isn't just an engineering nicety — it's a competitive investment, because it's finally something the market can see and reward.

The same logic extends quietly through the rest of a company. Engineering can say, and mean, the customer will be able to see this. So can quality control, customer service, and repair operations. All of them gain a little leverage they didn't used to have — not because their job changed, but because the market finally started paying attention to it.

What changes is that it gets harder to paper over mediocre durability with a great advertising campaign, once a customer's Genie can just go check.

Cheap Isn't Dishonest

Price still matters. So does convenience. Sometimes the $400 refrigerator is exactly the right refrigerator.

There is nothing dishonest about making an inexpensive product with a shorter useful life, provided the customer can understand what they're buying. An eight-year appliance honestly sold as an eight-year appliance may be perfectly good value for its market.

Cheap isn't dishonest.

Concealing what cheap means can be.

The Honest Advantage

Sawtooth doesn't need to beat its competitor with better advertising or drive it out of business. It keeps building good furniture, documenting what it does, repairing what it sells, and supporting products years after the sale.

Its competitor may have a perfectly legitimate market for honestly inexpensive furniture. Or it may decide to improve its materials, stock replacement parts, or become clearer about what its lower price buys.

Either way, something important has changed.

The Trust Economy doesn't require companies to become better. It changes the conditions under which they compete.

As verification becomes cheaper and evidence easier to find, differences that were once difficult for customers to see become easier to see. Businesses may respond by investing more in engineering, service, documentation, durability, and transparency—not because anyone commanded them to, but because customers can increasingly recognize and reward those investments.

The Information Economy became very good at rewarding whoever captured attention.

The Trust Economy adds another force: rewarding those who earn confidence.

Not because human nature changed.

Because the leverage did.

Chapter 24
Identity Is Not Reputation

Anthony was reviewing a new product proposal when Ben walked in and pulled up a chair without asking.

On the screen was a line of camping equipment from a manufacturer Sawtooth had carried for years — familiar name, familiar logo, the kind of brand nobody in the outdoor business would think twice about.

"We've carried them forever," Anthony said.

"They were bought," Ben said.

"The company?"

"That's what I'm trying to figure out."

Anthony smiled. "That sounds like a lawyer's answer."

"It might be an important one."

The brand name hadn't changed. The logo hadn't changed. Someone walking through Sawtooth's camping department would recognize the products instantly. But Ben kept scrolling through the acquisition filing. "Here's the deal," he said. "I'm trying to figure out what they bought. Did they buy the operating company? Or did they buy the name?"

Anthony stopped. Those weren't the same question, and it wasn't obvious to him, sitting there, which one mattered more.

Two Different Things

Every functioning economy depends on identity. Before trust can accumulate, people need to know who they're dealing with — a customer who bought a Sawtooth dining table a decade ago needs to know whether the company selling one today is the same company that made the first one.

Identity answers one narrow question: who is this?

A different question follows immediately behind it: what does their history give me reason to expect?

That's not identity. That's reputation — and the distinction stays invisible right up until the moment the two come apart.

When a Company Changes Hands

Suppose Anthony eventually sells Sawtooth. The stores stay open. The furniture workshop keeps building the same tables. The craftspeople stay. The buyers who select the camping gear stay. Supplier relationships continue, testing practices continue, warranty policies continue — the same people are still answering the same kinds of questions. There's a new owner, but there's substantial continuity underneath the name. Sawtooth's forty years of history still mean something because much of the organization that earned that reputation remains intact.

Now imagine something different. Sawtooth closes — stores shuttered, workshop shut down, employees gone, supplier relationships severed. A few years later, another company buys the name, the trademark, the mountain logo, and the domain, and starts selling products under the Sawtooth banner again, maybe even advertising "Sawtooth — Since 1987."

That's not the same situation, even though it looks identical on a storefront. The identity survived. The organization didn't. The new company might be excellent — it might make better furniture than the original Sawtooth ever did — but it hasn't operated since 1987. It has its own history to build, starting from zero, regardless of what the sign out front says. The old reputation was earned by the old organization, and it doesn't transfer automatically just because the name did.

Reputation tends to follow continuity of the organization, not continuity of the name alone.

A Truck That Says "Since 1972"

A homeowner whose air conditioner fails in August isn't going to spend two hours investigating a local HVAC contractor's corporate history. The truck still reads Johnson Heating & Air – Since 1972.

Maybe his parents used Johnson. Maybe Johnson trucks have been driving the neighborhood for decades. The name becomes a shortcut: I know them. But what does "them" mean? Maybe Johnson was sold last year as a going concern. Or maybe the original Johnson closed three years ago and someone bought the name and the truck decals. Today, distinguishing continuity of name from continuity of organization can take real effort. AI may reduce that effort dramatically.

What a Genie Sees

A Personal Genie doesn't have to stop at the logo. It can ask who owns the company now, when ownership changed, whether the operating organization continued, whether the people who produced the historical track record are still there. It might report back something like: "The company has operated under new ownership for several years. Most employees, facilities, and operating practices remained" – which suggests real continuity. Or it might say: "The original company ceased operations. Its trademarks were later acquired." – which suggests the identity survived while the organization behind it didn't.

Neither statement tells anyone what to buy. The human still decides whether that distinction matters to them. What's changed is simply that the distinction is now visible at all, instead of buried somewhere, difficult to find.

What Was the Logo Standing For?

Anthony leans back. "So the name isn't the reputation."

"No."

"But the reputation makes the name valuable."

"That's closer," Ben says.

Anthony looks out toward Sawtooth's showroom floor, the mountain logo everywhere — on the doors, the furniture tags, the employee shirts. He'd always thought of the brand as one of the company's most valuable assets. It was. But he finds himself asking a slightly different question now: what made it valuable? The logo never built a table. It never rejected a poorly made tent, answered a customer's question, or spent twenty patient minutes explaining to a first-time backpacker why the cheaper sleeping bag was the better fit for what he needed. People had done all of that.

Standards had done it. Experience had done it. The logo had simply come to stand in for it, over years, the way a signature stands in for a person without being them.

What Produces a Reputation

That's a question worth every business asking directly: what are we doing, every single day, that makes our name worth anything at all? Some of the answer is obvious — design, materials, manufacturing, quality control. A lot of it is quieter than that: a buyer who's learned exactly which suppliers not to trust, a craftsperson who catches a flaw before it leaves the workshop, a customer-service rep who's spent fifteen years learning how to solve the odd cases, a warranty policy generous enough that employees have room to make something right without a fight.

On a balance sheet, most of this shows up only as cost — payroll, training, inspection, supplier development. What it is, quietly, is the machinery that produces the reputation everyone agrees is valuable. That distinction matters enormously in an acquisition. A buyer paying for Sawtooth's name, goodwill, and customer relationships needs to ask a sharper question: what produced the reputation we're paying for? Strip out the capabilities that generated it — in the name of efficiency —and a buyer can cut costs and quietly destroy the thing they just paid for, in the same transaction.

What's different now is that this is getting harder to hide, because customers increasingly have a way to see the change.

What Happens to the Value of a Name

A familiar name has value partly because people associate it with what came before: *I know this name, so I have some idea what to expect*. But that shortcut becomes less useful when a Genie can cheaply discover what's behind the name.

As provenance becomes easier to discover, the reputation value attached to a name separated from the organization that earned it may fall sharply. The name may still carry recognition, style, identity, and customer familiarity. What it may no longer carry is an automatic claim to yesterday's reputation.

At the same time, demonstrable continuity — people, practices, standards, suppliers, and institutional knowledge — may become more valuable because it can increasingly be seen and verified.

A brand can be bought. Its history can't be. If the organization remains substantially intact, that history remains relevant. If only the identity survives, the new organization starts writing a new history — the sign out front notwithstanding.

Two Jobs of a Brand

Brand has long answered two different questions:

Is it good?

Is it me?

The first is increasingly answerable through evidence. A Genie evaluating a Sawtooth table can examine materials, joinery, repair history, warranty performance, and owner experience without relying on the mountain logo as a proxy for quality.

The second question is different. People choose things because they like them, because a jacket feels like them, because a chair belongs in the cabin they've imagined for twenty years. Design, heritage, aesthetics, and belonging aren't engineering specifications.

As evidence becomes better at answering is it good?, brand may increasingly concentrate on is it me?

And that may be what branding was always best at.

A Second Look at Leverage

This extends the "quality gains leverage" idea from the last chapter in a useful direction. When customers leaned heavily on brand recognition as a proxy for quality, an unknown manufacturer faced a real disadvantage, however good their product was — nobody knew, and a familiar logo could claim decades of borrowed trust just by sitting on the same shelf. A Genie changes that calculation. If a small, unknown manufacturer makes a genuinely excellent product, a Genie can examine the materials, the testing, the verified field experience directly. The unknown company still has to earn its reputation — nothing skips that step — but it may not have to wait decades for anyone to notice. At the same time, a famous name becomes somewhat less able to coast on recognition alone if the quality behind it has slipped, because the Genie can simply look past the name and check.

Reputation Isn't a Score

There's one more reason identity and reputation have to stay separate concepts, and it matters as much as anything else in this chapter. Reputation should never collapse into a single universal judgment.

Sawtooth doesn't have one reputation — its rustic furniture might have an exceptional durability record while its camping cookware is merely ordinary, and a newly launched tent might not have accumulated enough evidence yet to have much of a reputation at all. Different customers reasonably care about different things: durability over twenty years matters to someone buying a dining table; weight matters to a backpacker choosing a tent for three days in the rain. Flattening all of that into Sawtooth Reputation: 92 wouldn't clarify anything — it would just throw away the useful, contextual information underneath the number.

The same principle applies to people, and here it matters even more. A person's identity provides continuity — the person standing here today is the same one who made a commitment yesterday, which is what lets trust accumulate at all. But identity should never become destiny. People learn. People change. People make a mistake and spend years correcting it. Redemption doesn't require pretending the past didn't happen — it requires letting subsequent evidence matter just as much as the earlier evidence did. A poor decision shouldn't permanently define a company that genuinely corrected it, any more than one bad year should permanently define a person who spent the following decade proving otherwise.

Identity has to remain stable enough for trust to accumulate. Reputation has to remain open to revision. Otherwise reputation stops being evidence about what someone has done and becomes a permanent judgment about who they are.

Privacy matters here too. Establishing identity shouldn't require exposing everything someone has ever done. Different relationships require different evidence.

"What Would Someone Be Buying?"

Ben is still reading through the acquisition filing when Anthony gets up and walks over to the window overlooking the showroom — camping gear on one side, rustic furniture on the other, customers moving between them.

"If someone bought Sawtooth someday," Anthony says, "what would they be buying?" He answers his own question before Ben can. "The name's part of it. The stores, the inventory, the website. But that's not why the name means anything." He gestures at the floor below. "It's everything underneath it."

Ben smiles. "That's the expensive part."

Anthony laughs. "Apparently." He looks up at the mountain logo mounted over the entrance. For years, management had worked hard to make that symbol valuable. Maybe, he thinks, they'd had it backward the whole time. The job was never to make the symbol valuable. The job was to keep doing things worth putting a symbol on.

Chapter 25
Poisoning the Well

If reputation increasingly depends on evidence, then manufacturing false evidence becomes exactly the kind of thing a dishonest actor has every reason to try.

The Trust Economy will not eliminate fraud, counterfeiting, or deception. People have been finding ways to fake trust for as long as trust has been worth anything. What changes isn't whether deception exists — it's what becomes worth counterfeiting, and how difficult the fake becomes to sustain.

Counterfeiting Trust Is Nothing New

Civilizations have dealt with counterfeit currency, forged documents, adulterated goods, fraudulent credentials, and fabricated reviews for thousands of years. Whatever people rely on as a signal of trustworthiness eventually becomes something worth faking.

Sometimes the thing itself gets counterfeited. Sometimes it's the evidence around it — reviews, warranty records, test results. And sometimes the target is the institution doing the verifying: a fake accreditation body with an impressive name, official-looking seal, and no meaningful standards behind it.

Anything valuable enough to trust becomes valuable enough to counterfeit.

When Appearance Gets Cheap

Artificial intelligence makes convincing appearance inexpensive to manufacture. Professional writing, polished images, official-looking documents, entire websites — all of it can be produced in minutes.

That doesn't mean everything made with AI is deceptive. It means appearance alone becomes much weaker evidence of legitimacy. A beautiful website proves little. A professional-looking certificate proves little. A thousand glowing reviews arriving in a suspiciously narrow window deserves a second look rather than automatic confidence.

The same technology that makes deception cheaper also makes investigation cheaper. No person can reasonably check every certificate, every supplier, every test result they encounter in ordinary life. A Genie, in principle, can make far more of that checking practical — which is why, as appearances get easier to fake, independently corroborated evidence and verifiable provenance become more valuable, not less.

An Arms Race, Not a Final Victory

This book's honest expectation is that trust infrastructure will end up looking a lot like cybersecurity has looked for decades. Viruses led to antivirus software; defenses improved; malware adapted; detection improved again; attackers adapted once more. There's little reason to expect trust infrastructure will be any different. AI may make phishing messages more convincing — and it may also let a person's Genie examine a sender's history and context before anyone acts on it. Attack improves. Defense improves. Neither side wins permanently, and building toward a final, complete victory over deception isn't a realistic goal. The realistic goal is a system where deception becomes easier to catch, harder to sustain at scale, and less damaging on the occasions it succeeds.

Where the Pressure Will Show Up

The pressure will follow the value. If provenance influences purchases, provenance becomes worth forging. If certifications carry weight, certifications become worth copying. And if verification organizations themselves become trusted, corrupting the verifier may become more valuable than counterfeiting any individual claim.

Sawtooth eventually gets a firsthand lesson.

Sawtooth Gets Counterfeited

The first reports look ordinary enough. Customers are finding Sawtooth climbing equipment online at unusually good prices — authentic-looking photos, the right name, certification marks, glowing reviews, even documents that appear to show real testing.

Anthony studies the seller's site. "They've done a pretty good job."

Ben is already deeper into it. "Better than that." He pulls up one of the certification records. "They're learning what the Genies look for."

Anthony absorbs that. "Of course they are." That's the part that matters — the counterfeiters hadn't just copied Sawtooth's gear. They'd started copying the evidence around the gear.

Digging further turns up the cracks: manufacturing provenance that doesn't match Sawtooth's real records, a certification number belonging to a different product entirely, a testing lab with no record of ever running the test it supposedly ran, a suspicious cluster of reviews that all arrived within days of each other, product photos lifted directly from Sawtooth's own marketing.

"They didn't just counterfeit our gear," Ben says.

"They counterfeited the reasons people trust our gear," Anthony says.

A System That Learns

No architecture makes attack impossible. The better measure is resilience: how quickly an attack is detected, how far corrupted information spreads before it is contained, whether independent evidence can reconstruct what happened, and whether compromised credentials can be revoked without damaging everything connected to them.

Resilience doesn't mean preventing every failure. It means being able to detect, contain, learn, and recover.

Emma and the Offer That Doesn't Quite Add Up

Emma finds a great deal shopping online — good price, legitimate-looking photos, a seller with strong reviews. Everything looks right. Her Genie hesitates before completing the purchase.

"Several pieces of evidence conflict."

"What does that mean?" Emma asks.

"The product images appear authentic, but the provenance, warranty history, and supplier identity don't line up with each other."

"So it's fake?"

"I don't know. There's enough conflicting evidence that I wouldn't rely on the seller's claims without more verification."

Emma passes on the purchase. What her Genie doesn't do matters just as much as what it does: it doesn't declare the seller guilty, blacklist anyone, or broadcast an accusation. With Emma's permission, the suspicious evidence can simply be passed along to relevant verification systems for investigation, where other independent reports might confirm it — or might not. A trustworthy system has to be able to defend against fraud without collapsing suspicion straight into guilt. Those are genuinely different things, and confusing them creates its own kind of injustice.

Why "Poisoning the Well" Is the Right Phrase

Ordinary fraud has an immediate victim. Someone loses money, receives a counterfeit product, or has an identity stolen.

Poisoning shared trust infrastructure does something larger. If certifications become routinely suspect, every honest business has to spend more proving its certifications are real. If reputation systems fill with synthetic reviews, every genuine review becomes a little less valuable.

The cost spreads beyond the original transaction as slower commerce, greater suspicion, and additional verification.

Fraud harms its victim. Poisoning the well makes everyone pay.

Don't Build One Well

One response to all this would be to put verification under one powerful authority. That may simplify some problems, but it creates another: concentrating trust also concentrates the value of capturing, corrupting, or controlling whoever sits at the center.

A resilient trust infrastructure needs independent sources of evidence precisely so that the failure of one does not determine what everyone else must believe.

Forewarned

Nobody can predict precisely how people will attack institutions that don't fully exist yet. But we know enough about incentives to ask useful questions now.

What proves we're really us?

Could that evidence be copied?

Who verifies our certifiers?

If something we depend on is corrupted, do independent records exist that could help reconstruct what happened?

These aren't reasons not to build trust infrastructure. They're reasons to build it expecting attack rather than being surprised by one.

There will be snakes. Knowing roughly where some of them are likely to show up is most of what keeps you from stepping on one.

Chapter 26

Stewardship — A Civilizational Choice

Civilization is inherited.

None of us created the institutions, professions, standards, laws, knowledge, and infrastructure we depend on every day. We received them from people who came before us. We use them for a while. We change some of them. If we do our job well, we improve some of them. And eventually we hand the whole unfinished inheritance to people we will never meet.

Chapter 10 called that stewardship.

Artificial intelligence makes that old idea newly important, because many of the institutions that develop around AI may eventually exercise enormous influence over knowledge, commerce, verification, expertise, and human decision-making.

Someone will maintain standards. Someone will certify systems. Someone will verify claims. Someone will resolve disputes. Someone will decide whether a new method satisfies an established requirement. Those responsibilities require real authority.

The question is not whether institutions should have power. They will need power to do their jobs. The deeper question is what they understand that power to be. Is it theirs to possess, or theirs to steward?

Stewardship Creates Power

A steward is not powerless. Somchai had authority in his workshop. He decided how work was done, what quality meant, who was ready for greater responsibility, and whether a finished piece was worthy of the Beau-Teak name. The Master's Chisels were his to use.

But there was a distinction underneath that authority. He understood that they had come to him from people before him and would eventually pass to someone after him. He could sharpen them, protect them, use them, and perhaps improve them. He was not supposed to destroy them simply because they happened to be in his hands.

Institutions work much the same way, except the thing being held is harder to see. A standards organization may be entrusted with maintaining a standard. A verification organization may be entrusted with evaluating evidence. A professional body may be entrusted with defining competence. A government may be entrusted with authority that no private organization should possess. All of them need enough power to carry out those responsibilities.

But stewardship contains a boundary: the authority exists to serve the purpose. The purpose does not exist to serve the authority. That distinction can be surprisingly easy to lose.

When Guardians Become Gatekeepers

Institutions rarely wake up one morning and announce that they have decided to become self-serving. The change can happen gradually.

A standards organization needs technical expertise, so it invites experienced people from the industry onto its committees. That makes sense. Those people know the field.

Large companies have more specialists available to participate. They can afford to send engineers to meetings, prepare technical submissions, and spend years working through standards processes. Smaller companies often cannot. Over time, the assumptions familiar to the largest participants can become the assumptions built into the standard itself.

That does not necessarily mean anyone is corrupt. Industry participation is not the same thing as regulatory capture, and expertise from the people who actually understand a field can be essential to good regulation and good standards.

The problem begins when stewardship becomes difficult to distinguish from control: when alternatives cannot receive a fair hearing, when incumbent interests become more important than the purpose the institution was created to serve, or when the organization responsible for judging evidence becomes dependent on the people whose evidence it is supposed to judge.

The guardian becomes a gatekeeper without anyone necessarily deciding that it should.

Sawtooth Runs Into It

Sawtooth eventually encounters the problem in an ordinary way.

Its engineers develop a new durability test for one of its product lines. The existing industry test measures repeated loading under controlled conditions. Sawtooth's engineers think they can do better. Their method combines repeated loading with temperature and humidity cycling, producing something they believe more closely resembles years of actual outdoor use.

They run both tests. They document the methodology. They repeat the work. They send the results to the organization responsible for the certification Sawtooth uses.

The new method is rejected.

Anthony reads the response.

"Why?"

Ben scrolls through the committee notes. "It isn't an approved test."

"I know that. We submitted it to become one."

"They say the existing test is adequate."

Anthony studies the committee membership.

"Three of the five manufacturers represented here compete with us."

"They're also some of the people who know the industry best," Ben says.

"I'm not saying they shouldn't be there."

Anthony looks again at the rejected test.

"I'm asking what happens when they're the only people who get to decide what counts."

Ben doesn't answer immediately.

Anthony keeps going.

"What happens if this becomes the only certification Genies recognize?"

"They'd practically control whether we could sell."

That is the problem.

The institution is necessary.

Its monopoly over judgment isn't.

Design for When Stewardship Fails

There is an old problem hiding underneath this new one.

The designers of the United States Constitution did not assume that wise, public-spirited people would always hold power. They hoped for good leaders, certainly. But they built a system of divided powers, competing institutions, checks, and restraints because sooner or later power would also be held by people who were mistaken, ambitious, self-interested, incompetent, or worse. The insight is larger than government.

Institutions can be excellent. But civilization should not depend upon every important institution remaining excellent forever. That applies just as readily to the institutions built around artificial intelligence.

We should want excellent standards organizations. Excellent regulators. Excellent professional bodies. Excellent verification organizations. We should select capable people, reward integrity, and build cultures that encourage good stewardship. But the architecture should not require every future steward to remain good forever.

A bridge is not well designed merely because it stands when every component performs perfectly. Engineers ask what happens when something fails. Trust infrastructure deserves the same question.

Hope for good stewards. Design for bad ones.

Centralized or Distributed?

This does not make centralization inherently bad or distribution inherently good.

Centralization has real advantages. A single institution can establish consistency, coordinate action, resolve disputes quickly, and avoid expensive duplication. A capable central institution may be an excellent steward.

Distributed systems carry costs of their own. They can be slower. Institutions may disagree. Work gets duplicated. Competing standards can create confusion. Too much fragmentation can make cooperation almost impossible. Both architectures can produce good outcomes.

The difference becomes especially interesting when something goes wrong.

When authority is highly concentrated, the failure of the center can propagate through everything that depends upon it. When authority is distributed among independent institutions, one can fail while others continue. Distribution does not make the people inside those institutions wiser or more virtuous. It changes the consequences when they are not.

A distributed system does not require every institution to remain good in order for the system to remain good.

That is resilience.

Stewardship, Distribution, Resilience

Stewardship tells us how power should be exercised. Authority is held in service of a purpose larger than the institution exercising it. Distribution limits the damage when it isn't. No single steward should become unnecessarily indispensable to everyone else. Resilience tells us whether the architecture worked.

When an institution fails, becomes captured, makes a serious mistake, or simply grows obsolete, can the larger system continue?

Distribution alone isn't enough. Fifty bad institutions are not necessarily better than one good one. Fifty incompatible standards are not a functioning network.

The goal is not fragmentation. It is distributed authority with interoperable standards. Many institutions can participate, compete, disagree, challenge one another, and occasionally fail while still communicating through enough shared standards for the larger system to work.

Some redundancy and friction are not defects in that architecture. They are part of what makes it resilient.

Who Verifies the Verifier?

Verification institutions face another problem: they need to be trusted too. Today that often produces a chain. One organization certifies a product. Another accredits the certifier. Another authority recognizes the accrediting organization. Eventually the chain stops somewhere.

A Trust Economy cannot solve that problem simply by making the chain longer. The institutions that verify trust must themselves be verifiable.

Who funds them? Who governs them? What standards do they use? What conflicts of interest exist? What is their record? Can their decisions be challenged? Can another qualified organization examine the same evidence and reach a different conclusion?

That does not mean exposing everything. People retain privacy. Businesses retain legitimate trade secrets. Creators retain intellectual property. Security systems sometimes depend upon information remaining confidential.

The principle is narrower: People retain privacy. Power gets transparency.

The more authority an institution exercises over others, the stronger the case that the exercise of that authority should be inspectable. A steward should be able to explain what it did with the power entrusted to it.

Consensus Isn't Proof

Distribution creates another temptation. If one authority saying something does not make it true, perhaps agreement among many authorities does. Not necessarily.

Institutions can share assumptions. Experts can learn from the same mistaken source. An entire field can overlook something that one dissenter notices. The Trust Economy cannot simply replace *the authority says so* with *everybody says so* and call that progress.

Consensus can be evidence. Strong consensus among independent experts may be very good evidence. But evidence still matters more than headcount.

That is particularly important for innovation. Sawtooth's durability test should not become valid merely because Sawtooth says it is better. But neither should it become invalid merely because the established committee says the old test is good enough.

Run the test.

Examine the methodology.

Replicate the results.

Let the evidence earn the conclusion.

Exit Matters

Stewardship also implies something institutions do not always enjoy contemplating: They can be replaced.

If a verifier becomes unreliable, another qualified verifier should be able to take its place. If a standards organization stops serving its purpose, competing standards should be possible. If an institution becomes captured, people should not have to abandon the entire Trust Network merely to escape that institution.

This is one reason interoperability matters so much. Exit is only meaningful when leaving one institution does not require leaving the whole system.

A steward who cannot be replaced eventually stops being merely a steward.

The Chisels, Again

Somchai's chisels were easier to understand because you could hold them in your hands.

He received them from craftsmen who came before him. He cared for them. He used them. He added his own work to the tradition they represented. Then, when the time came, he placed them into his son's hands.

The institutions of an AI civilization will be harder to hold. But the obligation is remarkably similar.

Maintain what still works. Improve what can be improved. Protect what has been entrusted to you. Do not confuse temporary custody with permanent ownership. And leave the thing capable of serving people you will never meet.

The office belongs temporarily to the steward. The purpose does not.

A Civilizational Choice

Artificial intelligence will give people and institutions capabilities earlier generations never possessed. Some of those capabilities will become embedded in standards, verification systems, professional organizations, governments, and institutions we have not invented yet.

Those institutions will need authority. Some may be centralized. Others may be distributed. Both arrangements can work well. Stewardship is the principle that applies to either. And resilience is the test.

A civilization that depends on every important institution remaining wise, competent, independent, and benevolent forever has designed itself around an assumption history gives us little reason to make. We can expect better without depending on perfection.

We can build institutions worth trusting while preserving the ability to question them. We can give stewards enough authority to do their jobs without quietly turning temporary authority into permanent ownership. We can accept some redundancy, disagreement, and friction when those things make the larger system more capable of surviving failure.

Chapter 10 asked what each generation should do with the inheritance it receives.

Use it well. Improve what we can. Protect the ability of others to improve it after us. And when our time with it is finished, pass it on.

Artificial intelligence may give this generation extraordinary capabilities. What we build with them may endure long after we're gone.

Stewardship is more than a management philosophy.

It is a civilizational choice.

STANDARDS

Chapter 27

Standards —The Invisible Language of Civilization

Imagine ordering a table, and the manufacturer tells you it's thirty inches high.

"Whose inches?" you ask.

"Ours," the manufacturer says.

The absurdity is the whole point. Civilization couldn't function for a day if every company kept its own private system of measurement. A meter means the same thing in Germany as it does in Japan. A kilogram doesn't shift when it crosses a border. None of that happened by accident — it's an agreement, made once, that we now barely notice we're relying on. When someone says a board is two meters long, nobody starts negotiating what a meter is. That question got settled long before this particular conversation started. Standards remove questions that no longer need to be asked.

Already Everywhere

None of this needs inventing for the Trust Economy — it already surrounds us. Weights and measures, electrical voltages, barcodes, internet protocols. An accountant works within GAAP, an engineer may rely on ASTM test standards, and computers communicate because they share common protocols.

These standards come from different places — professional bodies, industries, governments, international cooperation, or sometimes nothing more official than enough people finding it useful enough to adopt. What matters isn't who wrote any particular one. It's what they all accomplish: letting independent people and organizations cooperate without first having to invent a shared language from scratch, every single time.

Standards Are the Key

Thousands of independent institutions are resilient. Thousands of independent institutions that cannot understand one another are chaos. Standards make distribution interoperable.

The internet is the intuitive example. No single company owns every computer connected to it. What makes the whole thing work is that independent computers, built by companies with no obligation to trust one another, agree on compatible ways to communicate. The same pattern can work for the rest of what this book describes—Genies, certifying organizations, testing labs, Smartware developers—all remaining independent, without common ownership, but with enough common language to understand one another.

Standardize the Interface, Not the Implementation

The distinction worth making is that standards can define what independent systems need to share without unnecessarily prescribing what happens inside them.

A plumbing standard needs to fix a pipe's diameter and thread pattern — it has no business telling anyone what the faucet should look like, what it's made of, or what it costs. A shipping-container standard fixes the container's dimensions so it can move seamlessly between a crane, a truck bed, and a cargo ship — it says nothing about what's packed inside.

The useful shorthand is: Standardize what needs to be shared for independent things to connect. Leave everything else open to competition and innovation.

This matters more than it sounds like it should, because standards themselves can quietly become instruments of control. A standard that defines how something gets measured lets an innovator like Sawtooth demonstrate that a new design genuinely performs better. A standard that instead prescribes how the product must be designed can foreclose the innovation before it's ever tried. One protects competition.

The other can, without anyone quite meaning it to, suppress it — which is exactly the capture risk Chapter 26 spent its own pages on.

It helps to think of the right layer of standardization as pre-competitive: a shared foundation that competitors genuinely benefit from having in common, because fighting over incompatible measurements or connectors creates almost no real value for anyone. Competition then does its actual work sitting on top of that shared foundation, not inside it.

"We Already Do This"

Anthony's first reaction to hearing about "AI standards" is to picture some alien new technical world Sawtooth will have to learn from scratch. Ben brings him back down to earth.

Sawtooth's products already carry standardized measurements. Its suppliers already work to standardized specifications. Its accounting already follows recognized accounting standards. Say Sawtooth publishes a spec sheet for a piece of cabin furniture — dimensions, materials, weight, finish, the testing method behind its durability claim, its repair and warranty information. If those fields follow recognized formats, a customer's Genie can simply read them, without Sawtooth needing to build any kind of special translator for every AI company that might come knocking.

"So we don't have to convince every AI company to understand us," Anthony says.

"No," Ben says. "You just have to speak the language everyone already agreed to understand."

Anthony sits with that. "So this isn't really new."

"The technology is," Ben says. "The need to agree on what things mean isn't."

That's the moment this chapter is built around — not a leap into something unfamiliar, but the recognition that the AI economy is extending a mechanism civilization has been running on for centuries, into a handful of new places that happen to need it now.

Three Related Words, Not One

Suppose a standard defines how rechargeable-battery life is measured. A laboratory tests Sawtooth's battery against it and certifies the result.

Emma's Genie can then verify the laboratory, test method, and provenance before relying on the claim.

The standard creates shared meaning. Certification records an evaluation against it. Verification asks whether the resulting claim deserves confidence.

Standards Have to Earn Trust to Stay Alive

If the institutions that verify trust must be verifiable, so must the standards those institutions rely on.

A Genie evaluating a standard may ask who issued it, which version is in use, what changed since the last revision, and what evidence supports it. A document doesn't become trustworthy just because the word standard appears in its title. The standards underlying the Trust Economy have to participate in the Trust Economy too, with their histories, evidence, and revisions open to examination.

Good standards also have to stay alive. Science advances. Technology changes. Experience reveals weaknesses nobody anticipated. A standard earns trust partly through stability, but it keeps that trust by improving when the evidence says it should.

Standards Build Markets

Worth underlining for anyone running a business: standards don't just reduce friction — they can create entire markets that wouldn't otherwise exist. Standard electrical systems let appliance manufacturers design for broadly compatible electrical service. Standard shipping containers let ports, ships, trucks, and cranes around the world participate in the same logistics system without ever negotiating with each other directly. Compatibility, in every one of these cases, lowered the cost of entering the market — businesses got to compete on quality, price, and service instead of competing by locking customers out of everyone else's ecosystem.

The same shift may happen with Trust Economy standards. Once common formats exist for specifications, provenance, repair history, and verification evidence, an entire layer of new services can be built on top of that shared foundation. That leaves today's business leader with a genuinely useful, immediately actionable question: what information about our company, our products, and our services will eventually need to be structured and machine-readable, so our customers' Genies can understand it? Nobody has to wait for the rest of this architecture to fully exist to start improving the clarity and consistency of the information they already publish.

What Emma Never Sees

Emma asks her Genie to compare three dining tables: one made domestically, one in Europe, and one in Asia. Their manufacturers operate with different currencies, supply chains, standards, and business systems. Emma never has to think about any of that.. Her Genie hands her one clean comparison: dimensions, materials, durability, repairability, warranty, expected service life, confidence in the evidence behind each claim. She picks the table that fits what she wants.

Thousands of agreements, made by people Emma will never meet, are quietly doing the work that lets her get one understandable answer. That's what a successful standard looks like when it's working. It becomes almost invisible.

Nobody thinks about a bolt's thread pattern.

They just expect the nut to fit.

A SECOND GREAT RENAISSANCE
PRESERVE
UNDERSTAND
DISCERN
INNOVATE
BUILD
FLOURISH

Chapter 28
The Living Library

One morning, Anthony walks into Ben's office carrying a failed hinge.

"We've had three of these fail in six months."

Ben turns it over in his hand. "Same failure?"

"Looks like it."

Ben pulls up Sawtooth's records — current warranty reports, then supplier records, then engineering reports, working backward through the archive. A few moments later, he stops. "Huh."

Anthony knows that sound. "What?"

"We've seen this before." Ben opens an old engineering report. Different supplier, different production run, nearly identical failure pattern. Someone had traced it, years ago, to a heat-treatment problem.

Anthony looks at the author's name. "Frank Delaney."

"Yep."

"Frank retired nine years ago."

"Yep."

Anthony shakes his head. "I knew Frank shouldn't have retired."

Every experienced business leader knows a Frank. He remembers why a tolerance changed, which supplier caused problems two decades back, why an apparently unnecessary step got added to a manufacturing procedure, the experiment that failed quietly and never made it into a product. Then

Frank retires, and unless someone happened to write it down, that knowledge retires with him.

Sawtooth didn't lose anything this time, because Frank had, fourteen years earlier, written his findings into an engineering report that never got looked at again — until an AI system searching Sawtooth's records could find it in seconds. That's the whole idea of this chapter, in miniature: the knowledge already existed. What changed was whether anyone could still reach it.

The Library Already Exists

None of this requires inventing something new. Civilization has been building institutions for exactly this purpose for thousands of years — libraries preserving books, archives preserving records, museums preserving artifacts, universities preserving scholarship, patent offices preserving inventions.

Wikipedia demonstrated something further: that a body of knowledge could be continuously revised while preserving citations and a visible history of how the record changed. The foundation of what this chapter calls the Living Library already exists. Artificial intelligence doesn't create civilization's memory. It changes what civilization can do with the memory it already has.

What AI adds is a genuinely new capability: it can examine enormous collections of records rapidly — not just searching for a keyword, but for meaning, relationships, patterns, and contradictions across material no single person would ever have time to read in full. A company might hold fifty years of engineering records, service reports, and correspondence, all of it technically preserved, most of it effectively invisible simply because nobody has the hours to dig through it. Search engines helped with part of that problem. Searching for a word isn't the same as understanding what's there. When the cost of exploring an archive falls far enough, questions that once required impractical amounts of research can become worth asking after all.

A Living Library is a preserved and maintained collection made accessible to AI-assisted inquiry, so accumulated knowledge can continue to be discovered and used.

Memory Includes the Mistakes

A Living Library worth the name doesn't just preserve whatever later generations decided turned out to be correct. Civilization learns from failure and disagreement as much as from success — Newton doesn't disappear because Einstein came later; an old engineering standard someone abandoned decades ago may be exactly what's needed to restore a building built under it; a scientific theory that turned out to be wrong is often essential to understanding why the theory that replaced it held up.

The point isn't preserving a tidy, retroactively correct version of history. It's preserving the actual path. The competing explanations, the disagreement, the evidence on both sides. So a Genie can eventually explain not just what's currently believed, but how it came to be believed, and what's still genuinely disputed. Civilization's memory has to include its mistakes, or it isn't really memory at all — just a highlight reel.

Storage Is Not the Same as Preservation

Digital does not mean permanent. Paper burns, molds, and fades, and yet a book kept on a reasonable shelf can remain perfectly readable centuries later using nothing more than human eyes. Digital media fails differently, and often more quietly. Magnetic drives degrade. Optical disks become unreadable. File formats go obsolete.

The software that once opened a file disappears, and eventually the hardware needed to even attempt reading an old storage medium disappears along with it. A perfectly intact file can become permanently useless simply because nothing left in existence knows how to open it.

Preservation, in other words, isn't a one-time act. It is an ongoing responsibility. Important records need to be copied, migrated to current formats, checked against their originals, and stored in more than one independent place, indefinitely, for as long as they're meant to matter. AI can genuinely help with this work. Flagging endangered collections, spotting obsolete formats before they become unreadable, comparing a migrated copy against its original to confirm nothing was lost in the move.

But none of that changes the underlying rule: AI cannot retrieve what civilization failed to preserve in the first place. It can only work with what someone, at some point, bothered to keep.

From Records Retention to Knowledge Preservation

Most businesses already keep records, often because a law, a contract, or a tax requirement makes them. AI adds a second, quieter reason: the records themselves may contain knowledge worth keeping, independent of any legal obligation to keep them.

That shifts the question a business ought to be asking. Not just how long are we required to hold this? but could someone learn something valuable from this later? Old engineering drawings, failed experiments, supplier correspondence, retired product specs, the reasoning that led to a decision rather than just the decision itself — all of it can end up mattering more than it looked like it would at the time.

Frank's fourteen-year-old report was never going to satisfy any retention requirement on its own merits. It turned out to be exactly what Sawtooth needed.

The practical question worth any business asking itself now: are you creating records today that your company will be able to learn from tomorrow? A future Genie can't learn from what was never written down.

The Librarian Doesn't Disappear

As organizational memory becomes this much more valuable, someone still has to take care of it, and civilization already has professions built around exactly that responsibility. Librarians, archivists, records managers, information scientists. Their work has never really been about shelving books. It's about classification, provenance, preservation, access, and the judgment to know what's worth keeping and how it should be protected.

AI produces something close to the opposite of what people usually expect here. AI may greatly expand what people can practically discover and use within the collections these professionals manage. The librarian doesn't disappear because a Genie can search. The ability to search makes good stewardship more valuable, not less.

Large organizations may keep their own archivists and knowledge stewards on staff. Smaller ones often won't have enough volume to justify a full-time specialist — which is where an existing kind of service, doing more of what it already does, fits naturally.

Companies like Iron Mountain already store and manage enormous collections of paper and digital business records; scanning services already digitize paper archives; cloud providers already maintain large repositories. AI mainly changes the economics of what those existing services can offer.

A future version might look like a cross between a vault, an archive, and a library. A smaller manufacturer sending decades of records to a provider that preserves the originals, digitizes what makes sense to digitize, migrates aging formats before they fail, verifies its own copies against the source, and lets the manufacturer's own authorized Genies investigate the accumulated record on request. The company still owns its information. The service is simply its custodian — records storage evolving into genuine knowledge preservation.

Preservation Doesn't Mean Permission

Not everything worth preserving should be available to everyone, and a Living Library has to protect that boundary as carefully as it protects the information itself. Some records are public. Some are internal. Some are confidential, legally privileged, or sealed by agreement for years or generations before anyone's allowed to see them. A family's donated letters kept private for fifty years, a company's engineering archive kept confidential until long after a product's discontinued, a government record released only once a legally defined period passes.

Preserving something and making it accessible are two different responsibilities, and an archivist increasingly becomes a guardian of exactly that distinction. Identity, authorization, and audit trails mattering as much as the underlying preservation itself.

That responsibility extends to the keys that unlock the archive. Encryption keys, recovery instructions, and authorization records may themselves require careful preservation. For a small number of critical records, the most resilient backup may be surprisingly old-fashioned: a protected paper copy secured in a vault. No operating system to become obsolete. No file format to disappear. No network required.

The future doesn't have to discard an older technology simply because a newer one usually works better.

For thousands of years, civilization has fought a long, uneven battle just to keep what it's learned from quietly disappearing. Artificial intelligence hands us a genuinely useful new tool in that old fight, not by replacing the library, but by finally helping us make full use of what is already sitting inside it.

Part IV

A Second Great Renaissance

Chapter 29
Human Flourishing

Markets, institutions, and standards are not the destination. People are.

If artificial intelligence makes civilization wealthier, faster, and more capable, one question remains, and it's the only one that matters: capable of what, and for whom?

The Trust Economy was never really the point of this book. Neither was artificial intelligence, automation, or efficiency, and neither, honestly, is trust itself. All of it is a means. The purpose — the only purpose worth building any of this for — is creating the conditions in which more human beings get the chance to flourish. Technology serves civilization. Civilization serves people. People remain the reason for everything humanity builds, including everything this book has spent twenty- eight chapters describing.

Now That We Can Do More, What Should We Do With It?

Every leap in human capability has eventually forced the same question. Agriculture let permanent communities form. Steam multiplied physical power far past what muscle could manage. Electricity extended the day itself. Computers accelerated calculation. Artificial intelligence is starting to amplify something further upstream than any of that — human cognitive capability directly. And every time civilization gains real new capability, the honest question that follows is never can we do this but what should we do with it, now that we can?

The easy answer is economic: produce more, grow faster, optimize everything. Those things aren't worthless. They're also not purposes — they're means, the same way a hammer is a means and not a reason to build anything. Efficiency matters when it lets people accomplish something worthwhile using fewer resources. It has nothing to say about what that something worthwhile is. For that, the question has to come back to the human being it's supposedly serving.

Efficiency asks how can we do this with less? Effectiveness asks a different, harder question: what are we trying to accomplish? A civilization can become extraordinarily efficient in pursuit of the wrong objective, and AI can make that pursuit extraordinarily efficient too. The Trust Economy, as this book has tried to describe it, isn't chasing an efficient future for its own sake. It's chasing an effective one — where greater capability enlarges what's possible for the people living inside it.

A Plural Idea, on Purpose

The Trust Economy doesn't define the good life for anyone. It tries to enlarge people's ability to pursue whichever one they choose. The Genie doesn't decide why you should live. It helps you live more capably according to whatever purposes you've already chosen for yourself.

One person wants to build a company. Another wants to raise children well. Another spends thirty years becoming an extraordinary cabinetmaker. Another takes up astronomy at seventy. Human flourishing

has never had one shape, and a book arguing otherwise would be making exactly the mistake this one is trying to avoid.

We Like Doing Things

For generations, predictions about automation have assumed technology's ultimate job is eliminating work. That assumption misses something people demonstrate constantly, almost stubbornly: given the choice, we keep doing things we don't have to do. People grow vegetables when the supermarket sells them cheaper. They knit sweaters a factory could produce faster. They restore old cars, learn instruments, run marathons nobody's forcing them to run. Competence is satisfying on its own terms.

So is mastery, and making something that didn't exist an hour ago, and solving a problem nobody made you solve. Technology, done well, may not liberate humanity from work so much as liberate people toward the work they find worth doing — and that distinction turns out to matter enormously.

The Apprentice's Joint

Years into Sawtooth's transformation, Anthony — older now — walks through the furniture workshop.

Apprentices work alongside experienced craftspeople; some will stay at Sawtooth, some will become engineers, a few will eventually start companies of their own.

At one bench, a young apprentice fits a joint by hand. Ten feet away sits equipment that could produce the same joint faster, and with more precision than his hands will manage for years yet. He knows it.

Anthony knows it. Neither says anything.

The apprentice checks the fit, pulls the piece back out, makes a small adjustment, tries again. This time it seats cleanly. He smiles.

Anthony understands exactly what just happened, and it isn't really about the joint. Capability has made this kind of craftsmanship more optional than it's ever been — nobody needs to learn this by hand anymore. And, strangely, choosing to anyway may have made it mean more, not less.

"I Made That"

Emma discovers something similar, on her own timeline. Over the years, she's built a table, then a bookshelf, and eventually carved a small wooden box for her granddaughter. Winnie helped throughout — explaining a technique she didn't understand, finding instruction when she needed it, walking her through which tool fit the job.

But Winnie never felt the grain give way under a hand, never had a chisel slip, never ruined a board and had to start over anyway. And Winnie never stood back from the finished bookshelf and thought, plainly: I made that.

What technology gave Emma here was something more valuable than convenience. It lowered the distance between curiosity and capability, between *I wish I knew how to do that* and *I'll learn.*

For a great many people, that may end up being one of artificial intelligence's quieter, more durable gifts: not doing things for us, but shortening the gap between wanting to learn something and being able to.

Why Childhood Shouldn't Be Optimized

This principle turns sharply important once children enter the picture, and it's worth being direct here rather than hedging.

If pure efficiency were the goal of education, AI would offer nothing but irresistible shortcuts. Why struggle through arithmetic when a Genie calculates instantly? Why learn to spell when it corrects every mistake? Why wrestle with an essay when AI can produce a cleaner one in seconds? Because education was never really about producing the answer. It's about developing the person who produces it. A child's clumsy, handwritten essay isn't valuable because civilization urgently needs five hundred more words about a novel. The writing is the exercise — remembering, organizing, choosing, revising, persisting, thinking. Nobody watches a child doing jumping jacks and complains that a machine could move their arms faster and more efficiently. The inefficiency is the point. A great deal of childhood works the same way.

Children need real time spent reading, building, arguing, failing, and getting bored enough to invent their own way out of it. They need to make things badly long before they can make them well, to feel real frustration and discover, on their own, that it can be overcome. They need other children, and adults, and the ordinary friction of being misunderstood and having to try explaining themselves again. Artificial intelligence will eventually magnify what a young person is capable of. First, though, they need capabilities worth magnifying — and that groundwork doesn't have a shortcut, however good the available tools get.

None of this argues for keeping children ignorant of the technology around them — that would be neither possible nor particularly wise. A child will naturally watch a parent ask a Genie about a leaky faucet, or help a grandparent trace family history, or use one to identify a bird in the backyard. AI can enter childhood the way plenty of other technologies already have: present, ordinary, not the whole environment a child grows up inside. Primary education can keep its center of gravity on the foundational human capabilities civilization has spent centuries learning to cultivate — reading, writing, arithmetic, speaking, listening, memory, making things, cooperating with other people —

while AI becomes a genuinely powerful tool as children mature enough to direct it rather than defer to it. The goal was never technological isolation. It's proper sequence: experience before abstraction, capability before assistance, human foundations before artificial augmentation.

Learning How to Learn

There's a second, more practical reason this sequencing matters. A world reorganizing itself around AI this quickly may move too fast for education to consist mainly of stockpiling a fixed inventory of occupational facts. A carpenter may need to understand new materials nobody's taught yet. An accountant may need to understand AI auditing that doesn't exist today. A sixty-year-old may decide, on a whim, to finally study astronomy. People are going to keep running into things they simply don't

know yet — probably more often than any generation before them. One of education's most valuable outcomes, maybe increasingly its most valuable one, is the plain confidence to say: I don't know how to do this yet. But I know how to learn. That capability alone may end up being one of the sturdier foundations of flourishing in the age this book is describing.

Learning How to Discern

Everything this book has built — verification, provenance, standards, certification, distributed trust — rests on one assumption that's easy to take for granted: the human being on the receiving end has to remain capable of judgment. A Genie can present evidence, trace where it came from, point out where credible sources agree or disagree, and make recommendations. It may even handle many routine decisions on a person's behalf. But the human being still needs the capacity to question its judgment: Does this make sense? — Who's making this claim, and how do they know? — What's missing? — What would change my mind?

That's not a soft, motivational-poster version of “critical thinking.“ It's part of the cognitive infrastructure this entire architecture depends on. If AI can produce ten plausible answers in ten seconds, people need to genuinely internalize that plausible isn't the same as true. If it can build an extraordinarily persuasive argument on command, persuasive isn't the same as correct. If a claim gets repeated by a thousand different sources, that popularity still isn't verification. The more capable these systems become, the more this particular human skill matters — not less. First teach a child to observe, then to question, then to reason, then to learn. Only then hand her extraordinarily powerful tools. Skip that order, and we risk raising people who aren't augmented by artificial intelligence so much as quietly dependent on it — which would be close to the opposite of everything the Trust Economy is supposed to build. A civilization resting on distributed trust needs citizens still capable of independent judgment.

That's not optional infrastructure. It's load-bearing.

Remaining Human

Every civilization has to teach its children how to become part of it through language, stories, skills, and values worked out through real relationships; not just information transferred but whole ways of being with other people. Artificial intelligence doesn't change any of that. The task was never simply teaching children how to operate the extraordinary machines civilization keeps building. It's teaching them how to be human, and how to stay human, while using them. Education built for this era shouldn't be preparing children to compete with artificial intelligence. It should be preparing them to remain capable people who can use it well without quietly handing their judgment over to it.

We have to teach children how to be human—and how to remain human.

An Inheritance Needs an Heir

Every generation receives things it didn't create — language, craft, science, custom, unanswered questions — and decides, generation after generation, what to keep, correct, or pass forward. The Living Library from the last chapter is more than a repository for exactly this reason: civilization preserves a woodworking technique, a failed experiment, a piece of music, a family's history, not because information deserves to sit forever on a server, but because some future person may need it. Preservation only means something if there's someone left, downstream, capable of receiving it — which is exactly why this chapter's argument about children isn't a detour from everything preceding it. It's the reason any of it was worth building in the first place.

What a Civilization Is For

GDP, productivity, and safety all genuinely matter. None of them, alone, describes a civilization worth living in. A flourishing one should also ask something harder: can ordinary people learn, build, and recover from failure? Can they participate in the institutions shaping their own lives? Can they discover what's true, preserve what they value, and grow more capable across an entire lifetime rather than peaking early and coasting? Prosperity creates possibilities. It doesn't supply meaning — people find that through family, craftsmanship, community, service, and the countless other ordinary places meaning has always come from.

We are not building civilization for the machines. We're building machines for civilization. And civilization exists for people.

Technology doesn't determine a single future on its own. It only creates possibility. Some roads from here concentrate power. Others distribute it. Some quietly make people more dependent on the machines and institutions around them. Others use those same machines and institutions to make people genuinely more capable. Artificial intelligence hands civilization extraordinary new tools. It does not tell us, and never will, which of these roads to take.

That decision is still ours.

Chapter 30

The Choice Before Us — A Second Great Renaissance

This book began with a water heater, and it ends not far from where it started: with an ordinary question, asked by an ordinary person, on an ordinary day.

Somewhere right now, someone is asking an AI which dishwasher to buy, or whether a contractor's estimate seems fair. They have no idea they're part of anything larger than solving their own small problem. They aren't, not really. But enough small questions like that, asked enough times, reorganize how a business earns its reputation and how an institution protects its own integrity.

Shopping led to verification. Verification led to standards. Standards led to institutions. Nothing in this book required anyone to plan that chain in advance. It simply followed, one link at a time, with people responding to a changing set of costs and incentives.

Capability creates possibility. Possibility creates choice. Choice creates responsibility. That's where this book has to end.

Not the First, Not the Last

Writing extended memory past a single lifetime. Printing multiplied whose ideas could travel. Computers multiplied how fast we could calculate. Each one, in its own way, already amplified human cognition. Artificial intelligence isn't the first technology to do that, and this book has no interest in claiming otherwise.

What may be different this time is scale. The amplification AI offers could be considerably larger than what came before it, which is reason enough to take the choices surrounding it seriously.

Not Humans Versus Machines

The public conversation about AI keeps framing itself as a contest — humans against machines, control against progress. That's the wrong shape for the actual question. The choice was never between artificial intelligence and humanity. It's between different ways of using the same technology.

A trusted Genie making a routine, delegated decision—reordering a filter, scheduling a repair—isn't diminishing anyone. The dividing line is whether the system, on balance, enlarges a person's ability to exercise judgment or quietly narrows it. Some systems will concentrate power. Others will distribute capability. Some will make manipulation more effective. Others will make it easier to spot.

The technology doesn't decide which. *We do*. One design choice at a time.

"I Liked You Better Before"

Going through old company records one afternoon, Ben stops scrolling. "Oh, this is good." He turns the screen around — an old Sawtooth ad, decades old: THE ULTIMATE OUTDOOR CHAIR, in letters large enough to settle the matter.

"Ultimate?" Ben says.

"Marketing wrote that."

"Apparently humanity had completed the development of chairs."

Further down: "'Built to last a lifetime.'"

Ben's Genie speaks up, unbothered. "Average documented service life: eleven years, seven months."

Anthony looks at Ben. "I liked you better before you had that thing."

Ben grins. "You said the same thing about accountants."

Business had changed. People, reassuringly, hadn't.

The Honest Transaction, Once More

None of this depends on people becoming better than they've ever been. There will still be exaggeration, still be fraud, still be people trying to game whatever gets built next. This book has never pretended otherwise. The Trust Economy doesn't assume honesty wins by default. It simply proposes that, as verification gets cheaper, honesty stops needing quite so much luck to hold up — and that shift, small as it sounds, is the entire wager this book has been making.

A Second Great Renaissance

A renaissance was never really about growth. It's a flowering of human capability across an unusual number of fronts at once. Artificial intelligence, used the way this book has described, holds the possibility of something in that family — not by repeating history, but by making genuinely scarce things newly abundant. Billions of people with real access to expertise that used to be expensive. Small businesses with capabilities once reserved for large corporations. People finding it easier to learn, build, investigate, and create — not because a machine did it for them, but because the distance between curiosity and capability got shorter.

None of that follows automatically from owning powerful technology. A civilization can have extraordinary tools and still grow poorer in dignity, community, and purpose. The measure was never the technology itself. It's what the technology lets people become.

Capability is not the purpose. It never was. Human flourishing is.

The Choice Before Us

That's the choice underneath everything in this book. Not whether artificial intelligence becomes capable — that's already underway, and no book needs to predict how far it goes. The real question is what we choose to do with whatever capability arrives.

Will it strengthen human freedom and agency, or will people quietly reorganize their lives around the convenience of the systems they built? Will children learn to observe and question before they learn to ask a machine for the answer?

These aren't questions engineers, companies, or governments can settle on everyone else's behalf. They will be answered one decision at a time—in the systems we build, the businesses we run, the institutions we steward, the children we teach, and the choices ordinary people make about how these new capabilities fit into their lives.

Everything Humanity Creates

A hammer exists because a hand wanted to build something. A library exists because people wanted knowledge to outlast them. A school exists because one generation wanted to prepare the next.

Technology has always belonged to that tradition. It was never the purpose. It's the instrument.

Which leaves, maybe, the simplest sentence in this book: everything humanity creates exists to serve humanity. Artificial intelligence should be judged by that same human standard.

We Are the Future

Someone, somewhere, is asking an AI a small, ordinary question right now, with no idea they're part of anything larger than getting today's problem solved. That's fine. That's how it usually starts.

I don't know whether this is the future we will build.

I wanted to show you it's a future we *can* build.

We are the future.

AI is here to help us build it.

Epilogue

The future rarely announces its arrival. It simply becomes normal.

❧

A young couple stands in a home-improvement store, comparing two water heaters that cost almost the same.

"Which one?" she asks.

Their Genie quietly projects a short comparison — verified service life, repair history, actual operating cost, warranty fulfillment.

He studies it for a moment. "So the cheaper one just costs less."

A pause.

"The other one's worth more."

The salesman just nods. He's learned there's no point arguing with evidence.

❧

A father is shopping online. His son watches over his shoulder.

"Dad, why doesn't this company publish their repair history?"

"I don't know."

The boy thinks about it for a second. "I guess my Genie won't like them."

His father laughs. His son is learning.

❧

The executive meeting has not gone well. Sales are down for the third straight quarter, and the CEO isn't in the mood for guessing.

"What changed?"

"Our recommendation score dropped."

"Quality?"

"No."

"Price?, Service?"

"No and no." The analyst turns the screen around. "Our independent durability certification expired six weeks ago. Nobody renewed it."

Nobody says anything for a moment.

"Renew it," the CEO says.

❧

A startup founder stands in front of a room of investors who are not, so far, impressed.

"How do you compete with companies ten times your size?"

She smiles. "They spend millions convincing people they're trustworthy. We're spending money becoming trustworthy." She clicks to the next slide — every supplier, every test, every field repair, every claim, independently verifiable.

An investor leans back. "So your marketing department..."

"Works for engineering. Mostly."

Somebody in the back writes something down.

❧

The commercial has no celebrity, no music, no narrator. Just a technician measuring moisture content, a lab signing a report, a customer running a hand over a twenty-five-year-old chair that still closes the way it's supposed to.

The last frame is only two lines.

Don't believe us.

Verify us.

❧

A man is helping his daughter set up her first Genie.

"Which reasoning system did you pick?"

"The open-source one."

He looks at her. "Why?"

"It scored about the same as the expensive one, and Uncle Ben says this one's easier to customize."

"Is it certified?"

She gives him the look reserved for fathers asking ridiculous questions.

"Dad. It wouldn't run on AIFIS if it wasn't."

"Just checking."

"Uh-huh."

❧

A retired electrician in rural Montana opens his monthly Smartware statement over breakfast.

His wife looks across the table. "Anything?"

"Hundred and eighty-seven dollars."

"For what?"

He scrolls through the report. "Mostly old houses. Somebody in Ohio used the farmhouse wiring module fourteen times."

She takes another sip of coffee. "Not bad for being retired."

He looks at the statement again.

"Guess some of me isn't."

❧

Years pass, the way they do.

Visitors still find their way to Beau-Teak Studio. Somchai is gone now — his son teaches there, his grandchildren help out, apprentices arrive from Thailand and from countries Somchai never once visited. Some come already knowing the story. Others learn it there.

On one wall, beneath a small wooden plaque, hangs a set of old chisels. Nobody uses them anymore. There's better steel now, more precise equipment, and, where it genuinely helps, a Genie quietly involved in the work. But the chisels stay exactly where they are, because a name can be inherited, and so can a business, and even a reputation can coast for a while on its own momentum. Craftsmanship can't. It has to be earned again, by someone, in every generation willing to do it.

What changed, in the end, was smaller than anyone expected and larger than anyone quite noticed happening. Businesses competed less on the biggest promise and more on how easy the truth was to find. Nobody declared a revolution. Markets just got a little better, year over year, at telling the difference between a good story and good evidence.

❧

Emma is older now. One afternoon her granddaughter comes to her, carrying two small pieces of wood.

"Grandma? Can we make a box?"

"A box for what?"

The girl thinks about it seriously. "My important things."

That settles it. Emma brings out a small tool chest — the same chisels she bought from Beau-Teak, years ago — and shows her how to hold one properly. Nearby, her Genie recognizes what's happening and quietly opens something like an Apprentice Mode: plans, measurements, a demonstration of the joinery, ready the instant anyone asks.

Emma looks at the wood. Then at her granddaughter.

"Let's try it ourselves first."

The Genie stays quiet.

The first line isn't straight. Neither is the second. Her granddaughter frowns; Emma laughs, and they try again. Only much later, when they reach something neither of them quite knows how to do, does Emma finally ask for help — and the Genie offers exactly one suggestion, nothing more, and goes quiet again.

The first lesson still passes the old way. Grandmother to granddaughter. Hand over hand, on a piece of wood that isn't straight yet.

Human to human.

Introduction to the Appendices
Further Ripples

The chapters followed the central path of the Trust Economy. These appendices explore what lies beyond it – possibilities the main argument didn't have room to develop fully, offered especially to leaders of small and mid-sized organizations who need to think about changing AI capability without an AI lab or a research staff to do it for them.

Some of what follows can be tried this quarter. Some depends on standards, institutions, or technologies that don't fully exist yet. Both kinds are useful to think with. None of it is a forecast.

A word on language: several terms here are deliberately invented – Marketeaching, Mindwright, Aitomotion, Smartware. Giving an idea a name lets people question it, budget for it, and build on it. The words aren't sacred. If better ones emerge, use them.

Appendix A
Capability & Talent

How AI May Change Hiring, Work, and Human Resources

The Job Description Problem

Sawtooth needed someone. Ben looked over the draft posting — bachelor's degree, five years' experience, CRM familiarity, presentation skills, a dozen other lines — and asked Anthony one question: "*What do we need this person to do?*"

It was harder to answer than it should have been. The job description described a kind of person. It didn't describe the results Sawtooth needed produced.

Hiring Has Always Used Proxies

Organizations can't directly observe what a candidate is capable of, so they use stand-ins: degrees, titles, years of experience, named software fluency. These proxies carry real information. The trouble starts when the proxy gets confused with the capability it was meant to represent. A company doesn't need "five years of experience" — it needs whatever judgment that experience is likely to have produced. It doesn't need someone who "knows PowerPoint" — it needs someone who communicates clearly. For most of modern employment, that distinction could stay comfortably blurry. AI may make it harder to ignore, because AI increasingly supplies pieces of what the proxy was standing in for.

From Jobs to Capabilities

Start from outcomes instead of credentials. What does the role need to accomplish — investigate problems, recognize patterns, coordinate people, exercise judgment, know when to escalate? Once the conversation is about capabilities rather than an imagined ideal applicant, a company can work backward: which capabilities must the person already have? Which can be taught? Which can be amplified by AI? Which can increasingly be supplied by AI outright? Which require human judgment or accountability no matter what AI can do? And — worth asking honestly — which requirements in the old posting were never that important to begin with?

AI Unbundles the Job Description

Traditional roles bundle many capabilities into one title: a manager who researches, writes, presents, budgets, and supervises all at once. AI can unbundle that bundle — supplying or amplifying pieces of it — which opens a genuinely different question for a small organization: does a capability gap require a hire, or does it require training, augmentation, better documentation, Smartware, or simply better tools for someone already on staff? A staffing gap and a capability gap are not automatically the same thing.

Glossary cross-reference: Capability, AI Leverage, Capability Stack, Capability Mapping, Latent Talent, and related terms are defined in Appendix B.

A Practical Exercise

Choose one position — ideally one the company is trying to fill now, or has always struggled to fill. Set the old job description aside. Start with a blank page:

1. What results do we need this person to produce?

2. What capabilities does producing those results require?

3. For each: must the person already have it? Can it be taught? Can AI help acquire or augment it?

Does it require human judgment or accountability regardless?

4. How would we know whether someone can do it?

Only then write the job description, and compare it against the old one. The differences are often the whole exercise.

The Larger Ripple

Industrial-era organizations learned to define work as jobs, jobs as titles, titles as boxes on a chart, boxes as requirements, requirements as filters — until, without anyone deciding it should happen, companies started searching for people who matched the filter rather than people who could produce the result. AI is an opportunity to reverse that sequence: start with the purpose, identify the results, determine the capabilities, decide which must be human, and only then find — or develop — the person who can responsibly deliver them. The future of Human Resources may increasingly be less about managing positions and more about discovering and developing capability.

Appendix B
A Language for New Possibilities

Sometimes We Need New Words to Think New Thoughts

An idea without a convenient name stays fuzzy—people sense pieces of it without realizing the pieces belong together. Naming it lets people discuss it, disagree about it, budget for it, and build on it.

None of the terms below are sacred. Some may eventually become ordinary. Others may disappear because someone invents a better word. What matters is the idea underneath the name.

New Ideas and Capabilities

Capability – the ability to produce a result. Not a job, department, or credential—those may contain or evidence a capability, but the useful question is always: *what must be capable of doing this? (Appendix A)*

Capability Mapping – identifying the results an organization needs and tracing backward to the capabilities required to produce them. *(Appendix A)*

Capability Inventory – an organized understanding of what an organization can do beyond job titles: knowledge, problem-solving history, unusual experience, and capabilities that could be unlocked with training or AI assistance.

Capability Stack – the combination of human knowledge, judgment, AI, Smartware, tools, procedures, and outside expertise that lets a person or organization produce a result. Two people with similar résumés can have very different effective capability depending on the stack behind them.

Capability Architecture – the deliberate design of how human capability, AI, knowledge, and tools work together across an organization; the answer to *where should each capability reside?* rather than merely *how many people do we need?*

Capability Gap — a need the organization cannot currently meet reliably. It is not automatically a hiring problem. The answer might be training, augmentation, Smartware, better tools for existing talent, or outside expertise.

Latent Talent — useful capability already inside an organization that is hidden, underused, or invisible because a job description, credential assumption, or old technology never called on it. The question isn't only *what does Susan do?* It is *what could Susan do?*

AI Leverage — the additional useful capability gained through effective AI use. Producing more output isn't leverage by itself; the test is whether something can be done better, faster, more accurately, or at a scale that wasn't practical before.

Continuous Awareness — an organization's ability to know what matters when it matters, rather than discovering it in a quarterly report. *(Appendix E)*

Attention System — an AI-enabled system that continuously reviews incoming information, identifies meaningful signals, prioritizes them, and routes them to the right people. Its purpose is Continuous Awareness, not surveillance. *(Appendix E)*

Marketeaching *(Marketing + Teaching)* — a business approach that helps customers understand a product's tradeoffs, evidence, and limitations well enough to decide well, on the premise that AI-assisted customers increasingly reward companies that teach rather than merely persuade.

AIFIS — the foundational identity and integrity layer of a trustworthy AI: whom it serves, its obligations, authority, and boundaries. *(See the appendix on AIFIS and IRIS.)*

IRIS *(Intelligent Reasoning & Inference System)* — the reasoning layer of an AI, distinct from its foundational identity. IRIS interprets evidence, weighs competing considerations, makes inferences, and exercises judgment within appropriate boundaries. Unlike the identity layer, an IRIS could potentially be updated or replaced. *(See the appendix on AIFIS and IRIS.)*

Smartware *(Smart + Software)* — organized intelligence: verified expertise, reasoning methods, standards, and Certified Knowledge Packages that help a person or AI think about or perform something well. Software provides functionality; Smartware provides capability.

Certified Knowledge Package / CERMOD — a body of organized knowledge, or a verified reasoning module, whose origin, evidence, and limitations have been sufficiently verified for trusted use. A CERMOD may power one function inside a Personal Genie. Smartware can include CERMODs.

Prequeling *(Prequel + Reasoning)* — planning backward from a desired future: what would have to be true immediately before it, and before that, until the chain reaches something actionable today. *(Appendix C)*

Rippling *(Ripple + Reasoning)* — following consequences forward by repeatedly asking: *if this changes, what changes next?* Structured exploration, not prediction. *(Appendix C)*

Distributed Capability — the principle that powerful capability can be more resilient, and often more beneficial, when spread widely rather than concentrated in a few institutions. Personal Genies are one expression of it.

Genie / Personal Genie — a person's primary AI assistant: advisor, organizer, researcher, negotiator, and advocate, operating within fiduciary and authority boundaries. ***One person, one Genie.***

Human Capability — the knowledge, judgment, creativity, experience, and relationships a human contributes. AI may amplify these without replacing their importance.

Quality Leverage — the added competitive value quality gains once AI makes it easier for customers to discover, compare, and verify. Quality always existed; AI makes more of it visible.

Stewardship — the principle that each generation inherits civilization and holds responsibility for maintaining, improving, and passing it forward —including the technology it builds.

Thegn — an old word for a trusted aide who faithfully serves another, used here to frame AI agents as trusted aides rather than independent actors pursuing their own agendas.

Trust Economy — an economic and institutional environment in which AI substantially lowers the cost of evaluating claims, evidence, and reputation, so demonstrable trustworthiness gains economic value.

Trust Network — the distributed system through which verified knowledge, reputation, and Smartware can circulate among people, organizations, and AI. Its purpose is the spread of trustworthy information, not central control of it.

Verification-First — an approach that weighs evidence, provenance, and verifiability before accepting a claim. It doesn't require certainty; it asks whether there is sufficient reason to trust something for the purpose at hand.

❦

New Work, New Professions

New capabilities don't only need names. Sometimes they create enough new work that eventually we need a name for the person doing it.

Before automobiles, there were no automobile mechanics. Before the internet, nobody hired search-optimization specialists. A capability appears, problems emerge around it, and eventually somebody asks: *what do we call the person who does this?*

The following are not predictions. They're ripples: functions that may become valuable if the architecture described in this book develops, whatever they eventually get called.

Don't start with the job title. Start with the problem:

What needs doing, and why would an organization pay someone to get unusually good at it?

Mindwright *(Mind + Wright)* — constructs, tests, organizes, and improves specialized AI reasoning tools and Smartware. The work may combine knowledge engineering, domain expertise, verification, and testing. If Smartware becomes an industry, Mindwrights are its craftspeople.

Aitomotion Engineer *(AI + Into Motion)* — turns *AI ought to help us do this* into *this now works*. An Aitomotion Engineer doesn't necessarily invent the underlying AI, any more than an electrical engineer invents electricity. The value is in application: understanding the objective, mapping the workflow, selecting tools, designing appropriate human review, testing the result, and getting the system into actual use.

AI Auditor — independently examines AI systems, their controls, and their outputs. Does the system operate as intended? Does it follow policy? Can important conclusions be reproduced or examined? Does it systematically disadvantage certain people? Different kinds of AI may require different kinds of auditors—a customer-service AI and a tactical AI should not necessarily be audited the same way.

AI Verifier — establishes whether a specific claim, credential, or evidence package satisfies a defined trust standard. Is this certification legitimate? Was this test actually performed? Does the evidence support the claim being made? The role extends work already done by inspectors, auditors, laboratories, and certification bodies.

Documentarian / Organizational Librarian — captures institutional knowledge and manages the collection that results. Library and information science already contains much of the expertise this requires. AI may make that expertise more valuable, not obsolete.

AI Trainer — teaches people to work effectively with AI: framing problems, directing tools, verifying output, and recognizing limitations. As basic AI literacy becomes ordinary—the way "computer training" once meant teaching someone to use a mouse—the specialty may move toward increasingly advanced applications.

AI Capability Coach — helps an individual identify and develop the combination of human and AI capability that makes that person more effective. The objective is not simply *use more AI*. It is to discover where augmentation genuinely adds capability and where human knowledge, practice, judgment, or experience still needs developing.

Capability Architect — designs an organization's Capability Architecture: what capabilities the organization needs and which should remain human, be AI-augmented, be purchased as Smartware, be automated, or be supplied by outside specialists. *(Appendix A)*

Provenance Specialist — designs and maintains trustworthy chains connecting claims, records, products, and their origins. The work extends existing practices in quality assurance, supply-chain traceability, archival science, and verification. Its recurring question is simple: *why should anyone trust this?*

Smartware Publisher — brings specialized intelligence to market much as a publisher turns a manuscript into a distributed, supported product. The publisher may manage testing, quality, versioning, licensing, distribution, and royalties for domain experts who know their field but not necessarily how to package their expertise as Smartware.

Trust Investigator — investigates attempts to manipulate systems of verification and trust, combining elements of fraud investigation, digital forensics, provenance, and identity verification. Verification will probably remain an arms race rather than becoming a permanently solved problem. Someone will have to work that boundary.

The Names Will Change

Some of these names may sound perfectly ordinary in twenty years. Others may disappear before anyone prints them on a business card. The Organizational Librarian may remain simply *the librarian*. The AI Auditor may eventually become simply *the auditor*.

The title doesn't matter.

The function does.

New technology doesn't necessarily mean less human work. It often means different work. The printing press didn't eliminate writing; it dramatically reduced the labor required to reproduce it. AI may do something similar across a much wider range of human activity.

None of the language in this appendix is finished, and it shouldn't be treated as such. Use these terms, modify them, or replace them with something better.

When something newly possible becomes important enough to discuss but doesn't yet have a convenient name, name it.

The most interesting idea—or profession—of the Trust Economy may be the one nobody has thought to name yet.

Appendix C
The 2-2-2 Causal Reasoning Framework

Exploring Possibilities Before Choosing a Path

Prediction asks what will happen. Causal reasoning asks if this happens, what might happen next, and why. That is a different, more useful question for a business that has to act under real uncertainty. The 2-2-2 framework organizes that question into three pairs.

2 Present Conditions

- **Position** — Where are we now? What are people doing, what technologies are already common, what habits and assumptions are built into the current system?

- **Capability** — What can now be done? This matters especially during technological change, because capability can shift faster than behavior does. A customer may already be capable of comparing dozens of products in minutes, while a business keeps marketing as though they can't.

2 Primary Behavioral Tendencies

Not laws — tendencies, useful as starting points rather than guarantees.

- **Convenience** — What has become easier or harder? People often favor less effort when alternatives look otherwise similar — though they also climb mountains and raise children on purpose, so convenience is a tendency, not an explanation.

- **Incentives** — What has become more or less rewarding, costly, or risky? Money is one incentive among many — time, status, security, and avoided loss all count.

When Convenience and Incentives point the same direction, that's usually where behavior shifts — and where it's worth Rippling forward to see what follows.

2 Causal Directions

- **Prequeling** — Start with a desired future and ask what would have to be true immediately before it, then before that, until the chain reaches something doable today.

- **Rippling** — Start with a change or possibility and ask what else it could change. Follow those consequences outward in every relevant direction, then ask what each of those changes might produce. Ripples may branch, intersect, reinforce or weaken one another, and sometimes return to alter the conditions that produced them.

Ripple Before You Choose

A possibility does not have to become reality before you can ripple it. If a new capability creates several possible paths, follow each one forward before deciding which to take. An attractive first step

may lead toward consequences you don't want. A less obvious choice may open possibilities you hadn't considered.

Once a choice is made, conditions change. That creates a new Position, often with new Capabilities, new incentives, and new possibilities. Then the process begins again.

Possibilities → Ripple → Choice → New Position → Repeat.

A Worked Business Example

A small manufacturer realizes AI can review every customer-service conversation, review, and warranty claim it receives.

Position: customer information is already collected, but scattered across email, CRM, reviews, and memory — management sees only a fraction of it.

Capability: AI can now categorize this material and detect recurring themes.

Convenience: what once took many hours of manual review now takes little.

Incentives: catching a defect early saves money; recurring confusion reduces returns. Real reasons to pay attention.

Ripple: the company starts noticing patterns → wants them surfaced automatically → builds toward an Attention System → problems get caught earlier → competitors eventually follow → responsiveness becomes an expected baseline.

Prequel: working backward from "we want Continuous Awareness," the company needs an Attention System, which needs reliable access to its information streams, which needs consistent collection, producing an action list it can start on today.

Use It Yourself

Pick one real change — AI or otherwise. Write the six questions on a whiteboard: Position, Capability, Convenience, Incentives, Ripple, Prequel. Don't aim to be right immediately. Branch the ripple, invite disagreement, ask what's missing. Look for an opportunity, a risk, or something you can start doing now.

Not Prediction

2-2-2 will not tell you what 2035 looks like, and it isn't meant to. It is a framework that you can use to explore multiple possibilities without committing to any of them. It's meant to help you make a better decision today. It's a place to start, a way to ask better questions, and occasionally a way to notice the first ripple before everyone else notices the wave.

Appendix D
The Evidence-Ready Business

Preparing for the AI-Assisted Customer

For most businesses, the AI customer won't be an AI. It'll be a person with one. The customer still buys the boots, the refrigerator, the insurance policy. What changes is their ability to investigate before deciding — and for most of commercial history, the business held the information advantage in that exchange. AI can narrow it.

Not an Expert — Better-Equipped

This doesn't require customers to become engineers or physicians. Their AI can explain which specifications matter, summarize thousands of reviews, and explain what a certification does and doesn't verify. The result isn't an omniscient customer. It's a better-equipped one — which changes the value of the information a business holds.

Evidence Becomes Part of the Product

Two companies both claim "built for years of outdoor use." One offers a photo and the claim. The other offers materials specs, test methodology, weight capacity, warranty experience, and known limitations.

Most customers today won't dig through the second company's documentation. Their AI might. This isn't new — aerospace components have long traveled with documentation because a functional- looking part with uncertain provenance can be worthless. What's changing is the economics: as the cost of examining evidence falls, practices once justified only for high-value transactions become useful much further down-market. A camping stove doesn't need aircraft-level documentation. The underlying principle still applies: the object has characteristics; evidence makes them trustworthy.

Start With Claims

Look at your own website, packaging, and sales scripts. For every claim — "premium quality,"

"professional grade," "built to last" — ask: what does this mean? What evidence supports it?

Could an intelligent outsider evaluate that evidence? Some claims hold up. Some are subjective and should stay that way. Some are inherited marketing language nobody's questioned in years.

Provenance Matters

"Tested to 500 pounds" is a claim. "Tested to 500 pounds — March 2024, ASTM method, independent lab, current production run" is evidence. The gap between the two is provenance: who did the test, when, using what method, on which version of the product. AI makes provenance far cheaper to examine, which raises its value.

Don't Hide the Limitations

AI-assisted customers may ask about weaknesses as readily as strengths: where doesn't this work well, who shouldn't buy it, what does the warranty exclude. Companies willing to answer clearly often gain credibility precisely because they answered. Sometimes the strongest sales statement is this probably

isn't the best choice for you — a customer who hears that when it's true listens much harder the next time you say this one is.

Customer Experience Is Evidence Too

Returns, warranty claims, support calls, and repeat purchases already generate evidence — it's just scattered across departments that don't talk to each other. An Attention System (Appendix E) can begin connecting those signals into a genuine evidence base.

Evidence Has a Lifecycle

A test from five years ago may no longer describe today's product. Evidence needs to be created, dated, connected to the claim it supports, reviewed, updated, and retired when it's no longer valid — which is part of why the Living Library (Appendix F) matters here too.

Make It Machine-Readable

A beautiful website that buries specifications inside images and unlabeled PDFs is hard for an AI to interpret reliably. You don't need to know today's future data standard to start: use consistent names, date your evidence, preserve originals, avoid burying essential facts. Good information hygiene now makes future machine-readability much easier.

The Evidence-Readiness Audit

Choose one product or important claim and examine six areas:

1. Claims — What are we saying? Objective or subjective? Does it drive purchasing?

2. Evidence — What supports it? Is the evidence strong enough for how much the claim matters?

3. Provenance — Who produced it, when, using what method, on which version?

4. Accessibility — Can a customer, employee, or AI system find it?

5. Currency — Is it still valid, or has the product or supplier changed since?

6. Gaps — What can't we answer well? Those gaps are opportunities — for testing, documentation, or sometimes for improving the product itself.

Start With One Product

Don't try to make the whole company Evidence-Ready at once. Pick one product, map its claims, find or build the evidence, and watch what happens — does sales use it, does customer service improve, does the company learn something about its own product it didn't know? If it creates value, expand it.

This work often improves the business before it improves a single sale: evidence gathered to earn trust frequently turns out to be evidence management needed anyway.

The Honest Advantage, Briefly

An Evidence-Ready marketplace exposes weak products along with strong ones — that's part of its value, not a side effect to avoid. A small manufacturer can't outspend a multinational on advertising, but if its product is genuinely better and that difference becomes discoverable, it gains something it didn't have before. (Fuller treatment in Chapter 23.)

Begin Before You Need It

Nobody knows exactly how fast AI-assisted purchasing will spread, and some of this book's specifics will turn out wrong. None of that requires certainty to start: know what you claim, know why you believe it, preserve the evidence, and be willing to acknowledge limitations. These are good business practices today. If the Trust Economy develops as described, they become competitive infrastructure.

A Final Note

Someone should own the system—not necessarily as a full-time job, but as an explicit responsibility. That person makes sure important claims remain connected to their evidence, provenance is preserved, outdated evidence is retired or updated, and the process doesn't quietly die once the initial project is over.

Appendix E

Building an Attention System

From Information Overload to Continuous Awareness

Most organizations don't suffer from too little information. They suffer from too little attention. Customer calls, reviews, returns, warranty claims, and employee observations all arrive somewhere — the problem is that nobody sees all of it, and nobody could. An Attention System is how AI helps answer a narrower question than *how do we collect information*; it is which information deserves someone's attention?

You Probably Already Have the Sensors

Most businesses already have what an Attention System needs: customers, employees, reviews, returns, warranty claims, CRM notes. The gap usually isn't sensing — it's connecting the signals. One rep hears a complaint twice this week. A salesperson hears something similar. Two reviews mention it. None of these individually looks important. Together, they may describe an emerging problem no single person could have seen.

The Cycle: Listen → Detect → Prioritize → Route → Review → Act → Learn

• **Listen** — identify the information streams already available and legitimately usable. Don't start by collecting everything; start with what you already have.

• **Detect** — look for repetition, unusual events, sentiment shifts, and unexpected praise as well as complaints. A sudden compliment about a minor feature is a signal too.

• **Prioritize** — weigh severity, frequency, safety implications, and reversibility. A credible safety concern needs immediate attention; twenty minor packaging complaints can wait for a weekly review. The goal is better attention, not more alerts.

- **Route** — send the signal to the right person. A possible safety issue goes to senior management and quality; a recurring instruction problem goes to customer service and documentation.

Information sent to the wrong person is often equivalent to information never sent.

- **Human Review** — AI identifies patterns and estimates significance. A person still decides whether it's real, who investigates, and whether to act.

- **Act** — someone owns the next step, or consciously decides no action is needed — and the decision gets recorded.

- **Learn** — was the signal important? Routed correctly? Did the action solve it? The system improves as the organization learns what it considers important.

Start With Customer Feedback

Choose a few existing sources — emails, reviews, support conversations, returns. Ask AI to surface recurring complaints, recurring praise, and anything unusual. Produce a simple report for one responsible manager, weekly. Ask: did this tell us anything we didn't already know? If not, improve it.

If yes, add one more source and repeat. This is how an Attention System grows organically, without a large upfront project.

The Attention Meeting

A short, focused recurring meeting — not another status update — asking: what is the organization noticing? What's new, what deserves investigation, what can be closed? A good Attention System should make this meeting shorter over time, not longer.

The Forgotten Sensor: Employees

Businesses sometimes buy elaborate monitoring systems while ignoring the warehouse worker who's already noticed a supplier's boxes arriving damaged. The problem is usually not that employees fail to notice — it's that the organization has no easy way for an observation to travel. An Attention System should give that observation somewhere to go.

Attention Is a Scarce Resource

AI can make information abundant. It doesn't make human attention abundant — a CEO still has twenty-four hours in a day. The point of an Attention System isn't providing managers with more information. It's directing limited attention toward where human judgment creates value.

A Pilot You Can Run Now

Pick one narrow area — customer complaints work well. Identify where they already appear (email, phone, reviews, returns). Collect a manageable sample from what you legitimately already have. Ask AI to find recurring issues, new issues, and possible severity. Have a human review the results and note what was useful, obvious, or wrong. Route one type of signal to one owner. Record what happened.

Add another source only when there's a reason to.

This is a genuinely high-value, relatively low-cost, relatively low-risk starting point for a business new to AI — it doesn't require autonomous agents or replacing anyone, and it can begin as a modest experiment: transcribe conversations, categorize them, look for repetition, route a weekly summary.

The useful question to keep asking isn't how much data did we collect — it's what are we noticing now that we weren't capable of noticing before? If the answer is nothing, the investment isn't creating value yet. If the answer is we caught a defect three weeks earlier or we discovered why customers keep returning something — that's Continuous Awareness working.

A Final Note

Someone should own the system—not necessarily as a full-time job, but as an explicit responsibility.

Appendix F

The Living Library Starter Guide

Preserving What Your Organization Knows

A fuller architectural discussion is in Chapter 28. This appendix is a practical starting point for a single organization.

Every organization has a library. Most don't call it that — it's scattered across file cabinets, shared drives, old email, and people's memory. Some of it is duplicated, some obsolete, and some exists only in one place: inside someone's head.

The Monday-Morning Question

What would hurt us if Susan retired tomorrow? Susan may know why a procedure changed ten years ago, which supplier can solve an unusual problem, or where the original drawings are. Everyone knows Susan knows these things, so nobody writes them down. Then Susan retires, and six months later someone asks why do we do it this way? — and nobody knows. The organization kept the procedure. It lost the reason.

The Knowledge-at-Risk Audit

Choose a department, process, or experienced employee. Ask: what do we know here that matters?

Where does it live — paper, a database, someone's memory? Who understands it — one person, several, nobody anymore? What would happen if it disappeared: minor inconvenience, or permanent loss? Can it be reconstructed, and at what cost? This exercise alone can reveal surprisingly fragile parts of an organization.

Capture the Why

Organizations are usually decent at preserving what they do. They're much worse at preserving why.

"Use Supplier B for this component" outlives the reason Supplier A's version failed fifteen years ago — and a new purchasing manager, seeing that Supplier A is cheaper, may unknowingly repeat an old mistake. Capture the decision, the evidence available at the time, and the alternatives considered, not just the conclusion.

Ask the People Who Know

Interview experienced employees — not with a hundred-question form, but a real conversation: what do you know that isn't written down? What do new employees usually misunderstand? AI can transcribe, organize, and index the conversation while preserving the original recording alongside the summary. The goal isn't replacing the experienced employee with documentation. It's making sure decades of experience don't walk out the door unnoticed.

Roles Worth Naming

A Documentarian captures the story of how work gets done — decisions, failures, lessons — not just procedures. In a small company this may be one responsibility assigned to someone good at asking questions, not a full-time role. An Archivist or Librarian decides what gets preserved, in what format, for how long, and who can access it — old questions that library and information science already has real expertise in, and which AI makes more valuable rather than obsolete. (Both roles discussed further in Appendix B).

AI Doesn't Eliminate Information Management "Just save everything and let AI sort it out" works poorly in practice. Six versions of a procedure and two contradictory spreadsheets are still a mess an AI has to guess through. Date records, name them consistently, mark what's superseded, identify what's authoritative. AI makes organization more powerful. It doesn't make organization unnecessary.

Preserve the Originals

An AI summary of an interview or test report is useful. It shouldn't replace the source material — interpretations can change, and future users may need details today's summary left out. Keep source material and interpretation clearly distinct.

Digital Is Not Permanent

Storage media fail, formats go obsolete, cloud providers change hands. Preservation is active stewardship, not a one-time save — important records need periodic migration and more than one copy in more than one place. And sometimes the most resilient format for something critical is still paper: it needs no software, no login, no update.

The Small-Business Living Library

A twenty-person company doesn't need a marble building. It needs: one well-organized repository, consistent naming, basic access controls, a handful of employee knowledge interviews, critical paper records preserved appropriately, backups, and one person responsible for stewardship. Sophistication can grow with need.

When You Can't House It Yourself

Not every organization has the space or expertise to preserve everything it should. Smaller organizations may increasingly use outside services combining secure records storage, digital preservation, and AI-assisted retrieval — a natural extension of records-storage and cloud-backup services that already exist. The company still owns its information; the service is its custodian.

A Starter Project

Choose one valuable body of knowledge — a major product, a retiring employee's expertise, an important customer relationship. Then: identify what exists, locate it, capture what's only in someone's head, organize it, establish its provenance, mark what's current versus historical, protect it appropriately, preserve it against format failure, make it usable, and assign someone responsibility for

keeping it alive. Then test it — ask someone who didn't organize the material whether they can find an answer, and why they should trust it.

The Knowledge-at-Risk Meeting

An annual gathering of people who understand the organization well, asked one question: what do we know today that we're in danger of forgetting? Retirements, system replacements, and closures are the moments knowledge is easiest to lose — and easiest to preserve, if caught before the transition happens.

The deepest purpose of a Living Library isn't storage. It's continuity — someone noticing what matters, before it's gone.

A Final Note

Someone should own the system—not necessarily as a full-time job, but as an explicit responsibility. That person makes sure important knowledge is captured, records remain organized and accessible, preservation and access controls are maintained, and the library doesn't quietly become obsolete once the initial project is over.

Appendix G
The AI Pilot Playbook

Start Small. Learn Cheaply. Expand What Works.

Don't Start With AI

Start with a problem: what takes too long, what do employees hate doing, what information do managers wish they had? Then ask whether AI could help. If the starting question is where can we use AI, you'll find impressive demonstrations that solve nothing important. If it's what problem is worth solving, AI becomes a tool rather than the objective — and sometimes the right answer will be not to use it. That's still a successful decision.

Look for High-Value, Low-Risk Problems

The best early pilots are usually boring: summarizing feedback, drafting internal notes, comparing documents, searching internal knowledge. Look for work where the benefit is real, an error's consequences are limited, a human can review the result, and the experiment can be stopped easily.

There is a startup cost, even when little new technology is required. Someone has to organize the information, establish the workflow, and develop the habit of maintaining it. For a time, that can create additional work before it begins eliminating work.

The Reversibility Test

Before launching: if this goes badly, can we easily undo it? An AI-drafted internal summary a manager reviews is highly reversible. An AI autonomously issuing refunds or making employment decisions is not. Early experiments should favor reversibility — learning is easier when mistakes are cheap.

Keep Humans in the Loop

The safest early architecture: AI proposes. Human reviews. Human decides. This catches errors, teaches employees what the system does well and where it fails, and builds organizational judgment instead of borrowed vendor confidence. Aitomotion should follow understanding, not precede it.

Establish a Baseline, and Define Success First

Measure how the current process works before introducing AI — time, accuracy, frequency —

or almost any new technology will look successful simply because the old process was annoying. Then define what "useful" (not "perfect") would look like, before the excitement of the pilot quietly redefines success for you; such as reduce prep time by half, catch a recurring issue earlier, reduce rework.

Pilot the Whole Workflow, Not the Demo

A demonstration shows AI producing a perfect summary. Real work includes obtaining the information, protecting confidential data, checking the result, correcting mistakes, and making sure someone uses the output. Measure the whole thing — a tool that saves ten minutes in one step while creating fifteen minutes of cleanup hasn't improved anything. Watch for this hidden work specifically:

correcting errors, rewriting awkward output, working around integration problems. Ask employees directly what new work the tool created.

Ask the People Doing the Work

Talk to the employees using the pilot: what does it help with, where does it slow you down, when do you ignore it, what would make it more useful? Employees often discover a tool's real strengths and weaknesses before management's dashboard does.

Don’t Automate/Aitomote a Bad Process

If five people review something only one person needs to approve, AI can make five approvals happen faster — the process is still bad. Ask why the step exists before automating it. Sometimes the best AI- assisted improvement is deleting a step.

Protect the Information

Before feeding organizational data into an AI system: are we permitted to use it this way? Does it contain customer, employee, health, or legally restricted information? Where does it go, and can it train another system? “It’s only a pilot“ is not a privacy policy.

Verify According to Consequence

AI can sound confident whether or not it’s right. A brainstorming list doesn’t need the scrutiny a regulatory filing does; a decision affecting someone’s job needs more verification than a draft picnic invitation. This is ordinary judgment, applied to a new tool.

Keep a Pilot Log

One or two pages: what were we trying to accomplish, what happened, what worked, what surprised us, what would we change. Six months later, someone should be able to answer what did we learn from that experiment — and the answer belongs in the Living Library (Appendix F).

Failure Is a Result

If a pilot doesn’t work, you’ve learned something cheaply. A small failed pilot beats a large failed implementation every time. The purpose of a pilot was never to prove management right — it was to find out whether the idea is useful.

Expand Carefully

When something works, resist “roll it out everywhere“ immediately. Ask why it worked — was the data unusually clean, was one skilled employee compensating for a weakness the tool has?

Understanding why something worked travels with the organization even when the specific software eventually doesn't.

Above all: don't bet the company. Run inexpensive, reversible experiments, because you cannot know in advance what will work.

A Final Note

Someone should own the system—not necessarily as a full-time job, but as an explicit responsibility. That person makes sure signals are reviewed, unresolved items are routed, the system remains useful, and the process doesn't quietly die once the initial project is over.

Appendix H

A Conceptual Architecture for Personal AI

AIFIS, IRIS, Smartware, and the Personal Genie

Chapter 15 established the concept: a Genie's identity and a Genie's reasoning are not the same thing, and shouldn't be built as though they were. This appendix is for the reader who finishes that idea and wants to know what it would take to build.

That reader might be a founder, a CTO, a product lead, an engineer, an investor, a standards professional, or simply someone who likes drawing boxes on a whiteboard. This is written for all of them. It is not a specification. Nobody has built this yet, and this book doesn't pretend to know exactly how future engineers will. What follows is conceptual engineering — the functions that should probably be separated, the reasons for separating them, the interfaces that likely matter, and the questions that follow once you take the separation seriously.

The Design Problem

A Personal Genie has to solve an unusual requirement: it should be capable of changing enormously over its lifetime without casually changing whose intelligence it is.

Its reasoning may improve. Its hardware may be replaced. Better models may become available. New Smartware may be added. A storage provider may go out of business. Some computation may happen locally, some remotely, on infrastructure that didn't exist when the Genie was first created. Through all of that, the Genie needs to remain — recognizably, functionally, legally — the same person's Genie.

The architecture this book has been describing addresses that by separating three functions: AIFIS establishes identity. IRIS provides reasoning. Smartware provides specialized expertise.

Each has different engineering requirements, different market dynamics, and different reasons for existing. Conflating them is where most naive designs go wrong.

AIFIS — Identity and Integrity

AIFIS is the comparatively stable foundation: who this Genie is, whom it serves, its fiduciary relationship, its authority and boundaries, and enough basic reasoning to understand and preserve those things. It should not be described as a rules file — it's closer to persistent identity than to configuration.

We don't know how it will eventually be engineered. Secure hardware, cryptographic identity, certified software running in a protected execution environment, or something not yet invented are all plausible candidates. What matters here is the function, not the mechanism: AIFIS is the part of the system that shouldn't casually change just because a reasoning provider ships a new release. It should be comparatively stable, secured, and resistant to unauthorized alteration — and there's no requirement that exactly one universal AIFIS implementation exists. Organizational, governmental, and tactical applications may require different implementations, configurations, or profiles of the same underlying principle. We don't know which. We can state the principle without pretending to know the eventual engineering answer.

IRIS — Reasoning That Can Improve

IRIS handles what AIFIS can't: inference, uncertainty, competing considerations, judgment, situations nobody explicitly anticipated. It reasons within the identity, authority, and boundaries appropriate to whatever it's serving — it doesn't get to reason its way around foundational integrity just because it's become more capable.

The interesting architectural move is treating IRIS as the layer where competition belongs. Different developers — commercial AI companies, open-source communities, universities, nonprofits — could build different IRIS implementations, each strong at different things: causal reasoning, conservative risk assessment, fast routine processing, clear explanations of the basis for its conclusions. We can't predict which categories will emerge, and this book isn't going to try. The principle that matters is: reasoning need not belong permanently to whichever company originally supplied the Genie.

That only works, of course, if components can interoperate — which implies standardized interfaces or compatibility requirements between AIFIS and IRIS. A hypothetical label like *compatible with AIFIS 4.3 and above* makes the concept tangible without pretending to be a real specification. This follows directly from the standards principle developed earlier in the book: standardize what must interoperate, and preserve competition everywhere else. Interoperability here doesn't mean uniformity — competing IRIS systems can reason quite differently from each other. The shared boundary just needs to be enough for each to function safely inside the larger architecture.

Open-source IRIS deserves explicit mention, and a caution alongside it: open source isn't automatically safer or more trustworthy. It would need to satisfy the same verification, compatibility, and integrity requirements as anything else. Its importance is architectural rather than moral — the reasoning layer doesn't need to be controlled by a handful of proprietary companies for this system to work, and commercial and open-source implementations could reasonably coexist and compete.

The formulation worth remembering: *keep your Genie. Change your IRIS.* A person might replace their IRIS because another one reasons better, handles uncertainty more carefully, runs locally, costs less, or because their current provider disappears entirely. The foundational relationship — the AIFIS layer, the person's accumulated context, the fiduciary obligation — should survive the swap.

Smartware — Modular Expertise

IRIS shouldn't be expected to personally contain the accumulated expertise of every electrician, physician, or attorney. Instead, it should recognize when specialized knowledge is needed and reach for the appropriate Smartware. This modularity matters practically: replacing IRIS shouldn't mean rebuilding an entire library of specialized capability from scratch, and adding new Smartware shouldn't

require touching the Genie's foundational identity. Reasoning, expertise, and identity can each improve on independent timelines.

Where the Genie Lives

A Personal Genie need not be an account that lives entirely on one company's servers. Its core identity could reasonably reside physically with the person it serves — the way a modern smartphone feels like one coherent device even though some of what it does runs locally and some runs remotely, some data lives on the device and some in the cloud. A Personal Genie could work similarly: some capability local, some remote, some Smartware installed directly, other Smartware accessed on demand, large models and Living Libraries queried externally as needed. From the person's view, it's still one Genie.

Its identity resides with you. Its capabilities may come from anywhere.

This deliberately avoids predicting specific hardware, storage architecture, or devices — those details date fast, and this appendix is describing an architecture, not a gadget.

The same logic extends to data. Some personal information may be stored locally; some remotely, encrypted, under the person's control rather than the storage provider's. Remote storage doesn't need to mean the storage provider can read what it's holding. That raises real questions worth naming without pretending to solve them here: who holds the encryption keys, what's allowed to leave the local system, whether a remote service can retain what it briefly receives, and what happens if a storage provider disappears.

Suppliers, Not Owners

Every external component — a remote model, a Smartware provider, a Living Library, a verification service — should be understood as *supplying capability to the Genie*, not acquiring ownership of it or authority over the person it serves.

The Genie may borrow capabilities. It doesn't borrow its identity.

This is really just the identity/reasoning separation applied one layer further outward — and it's central to why this architecture resists the kind of vertical lock-in where one company ends up owning a person's Genie, their reasoning, their specialized capabilities, and their data all at once.

Continuity Across Hardware

What happens when the device holding a Genie's resident core is lost, damaged, or upgraded? The hardware clearly shouldn't be the identity — but that raises real engineering questions a future team will have to answer, not this book: how continuity gets authenticated, what counts as the authoritative identity, how it transfers securely, how unauthorized duplication gets prevented, how recovery works after catastrophic loss. Naming these questions is this appendix's job. Answering them belongs to whoever builds this.

Security Boundaries Worth Naming

Separating AIFIS, IRIS, Smartware, and external services immediately surfaces a set of security questions any real implementation would have to resolve: Can IRIS modify AIFIS? Can Smartware alter IRIS, or AIFIS? Who authorizes an external model to receive personal information in the first place? What permissions does newly installed Smartware get by default? If an IRIS update materially changes behavior, can the user roll it back? How does the system verify Smartware provenance before running it? How does a compromised component get revoked? This book doesn't answer most of these — they're listed because separating functions this way makes the questions visible, which is itself useful. They're engineering questions produced by the architecture, not specifications supplied by it.

Different Principals, Not Different Instruction Sets

A Personal Genie, an organizational AI, a government AI, and a tactical system will have genuinely different principals, responsibilities, and authority. That doesn't necessarily require four separate reasoning architectures — it might mean different AIFIS implementations, different configurations, or specialized IRIS systems tuned to each context. We don't know which, and this book isn't going to guess. The principle that survives regardless: an AI should reason within the identity, authority, obligations, and boundaries appropriate to the principal and purpose it serves.

A Market Architecture, Not Just a Technical One

Separating identity, reasoning, expertise, storage, and computation doesn't just describe a technical system — it implies a market structure. An interoperable ecosystem could support competition among AIFIS certification services, IRIS providers, open-source reasoning systems, Smartware developers and marketplaces, Living Library providers, encrypted storage providers, and verification services, each competing within its own layer rather than requiring the person to abandon the whole relationship every time a better supplier appears somewhere in the stack. That's the economic core of the whole proposal: separable, interoperable components reduce vendor lock-in and concentrated control. A reasoning provider becomes a supplier to the Genie. It doesn't become the Genie's owner.

A Rough Picture

```
                         PERSON
                           |
   ────────────────────────┼────────────────────────
                    PERSONAL GENIE
                         AIFIS
                 Identity & Integrity
                           |
                         IRIS
                Reasoning & Inference
   ────────────────────────┼────────────────────────
        |                  |                 |
    Smartware            Living           External
                        Libraries         Models &
                                          Services
```

This is a conceptual separation of functions, not a physical system diagram — it doesn't claim that everything under IRIS runs on the same machine, or that computation flows top to bottom. It's a map of what depends on what, not of where the wires run.

Questions for Builders

Who owns the Genie's identity? What survives when its hardware is replaced? Can its reasoning system be replaced without losing the Genie itself? Can a person choose an open-source IRIS, and can any provider block migration to another one? Where does personal information live, and who controls the keys? What can an external model see, and what can it keep?

Can Smartware alter the Genie's foundational identity — and if the honest answer is "it shouldn't be able to," what enforces that? How does the Genie verify the provenance of a capability before it uses it? What happens when a supplier disappears? How does a compromised component get revoked? What, exactly, constitutes continuity of the same Genie across all of this change?

And underneath all of them, the question that matters:

Does this architecture make the person more capable — or more dependent on whoever built it?

This book isn't going to answer that one. Whoever builds this will answer it, one design decision at a time — and the answer will show up less in any founding document than in what the architecture quietly makes easy, and what it quietly makes hard.

Appendix I

AIVO — AI Visibility Optimization

A Sawtooth Story

Ben wasn't trying to invent anything. He was just bored on a Tuesday afternoon, waiting for a report to finish generating, so he decided to see what would happen if he shopped for a tent the way an actual customer would. He typed:

I need a good backpacking tent, something reliable, under four pounds. What would you recommend?

Three names came back. Sawtooth wasn't one of them.

He tried again, tweaking the budget. Still nothing. He tried a third time, mentioning durability specifically, and there it was — Sawtooth's three-season tent, third on the list, described accurately enough, recommended without much enthusiasm.

"Huh", he said, thinking. Not wrong, exactly. Just not the first thing anyone would grab.

He might have left it there, but he wasn't the kind of person who could leave a strange result alone. Instead of trying another prompt, he tried something that hadn't occurred to him until that exact moment.

Why wasn't Sawtooth in your first answer?

The AI told him. Politely. At length. And — this was the part that caught his attention — usefully. It hadn't found independent weight verification for the tent. It had less confidence in the durability claims than in the competitors', because the competitors had published test data and Sawtooth hadn't. It wasn't that Sawtooth's tent was worse. It was that the AI genuinely didn't have enough to go on.

Ben sat back in his chair.

It's not just answering me, he thought. It'll tell me why, if I ask.

He spent the rest of the afternoon poking at it from different angles, not entirely sure what he was doing, which is usually how Ben's best ideas started.

Susan Changes the Question

Susan found him still it three days later, muttering at his screen. She ran Customer Service with two full-timers and five part-timers, most of them retired outdoors enthusiasts who knew more about camping gear than the people designing it. She read over his shoulder for a minute.

"What are you doing?"

"Trying to figure out why AI doesn't recommend us as much as it should."

"Who are you pretending to be?"

Ben blinked. "What do you mean?"

"When I'm on the phone," Susan said, "I can tell in about four seconds whether I'm talking to somebody who's camped their whole life or somebody whose kids just asked to go camping and they have no idea what they're doing. They want completely different things. I'd bet your AI thingy can tell the difference too, if you gave it a real person to be instead of just", waving at his screen, "a guy typing 'good tent'. "

Ben looked at what he'd typed: `Good tent`. He'd been asking a machine to be a customer without giving it a customer to be.

That was the whole thing, right there, and it took Susan about eleven seconds to see it.

The Secret Shoppers

They built their first one that afternoon, and it was terrible.

Ben's first attempt read like a spec sheet with a pulse: `Experienced backpacker, prioritizes pack weight under three pounds, seeks` four-season durability rating above 3.5, budget flexible up to $600, requires seam-taped waterproofing.

Peggy — another of Susan's retirees, sharp as anything, allergic to nonsense — read it over Ben's shoulder and snorted.

"Nobody shops like that."

"It's accurate," Ben said.

"It's a checklist. You already decided what she's going to buy. You just dressed it up as a person." Peggy tapped the screen. "Give her a life. Not an answer."

They tried again. This time Peggy dictated, and Ben typed: Diane, fifty-four, has been backpacking for twenty years, mostly solo trips in the Cascades. Her old tent failed on her last trip. A pole snapped in wind, not user error, just old age. And she's shaken by it. She doesn't trust flashy marketing anymore. She wants something that will hold up when it matters, and she's willing to carry an extra half pound for that peace of mind. She doesn't know the latest fabric technologies and doesn't especially care to learn.

Ben ran it. The AI's answer came back completely different — different tone, different tradeoffs weighed, different tent recommended entirely. Sawtooth appeared this time, second on the list, with a note about repairability that Ben hadn't even known the AI could find.

"See," Peggy said. "Give it a person, not a spec sheet."

Enter the CIA

John had been watching from two desks over for most of this, not saying much, which was fairly normal for John. He was a retired Marine Master Gunnery Sergeant, most of his 30 year career spent doing intelligence work nobody at Sawtooth had ever asked him much about, because at Sawtooth he was just the guy who knew everything about backcountry gear and was patient with nervous first-timers on the phone.

He finally rolled his chair over.

"You know what you're doing — right?"

"Building customer profiles," Ben said.

"You're running an intelligence operation." John said it the way a person points out something obvious that everyone else has somehow missed. "You've got a target — what does AI know and believe about us. You've got sources — the AI itself, plus whatever it's pulling from. You're testing assumptions, cross-checking claims, looking for gaps in the evidence." He shrugged. "That's the job. I just used to do it about people who were trying to kill Marines instead of people trying to buy a tent."

Nobody said anything for a second.

"We're basically running a CIA," Peggy said. "The Customer Intelligence Agency."

That was it. That was all it took. By Thursday there was a hand-lettered sign taped to the break room door — CIA HEADQUARTERS — and by Friday Peggy had shown up with two pairs of drugstore sunglasses, because, as she pointed out with total seriousness, all spies wear them. Somebody found a rubber stamp from a garage sale that said CONFIDENTIAL and started stamping the printouts, mostly upside down, mostly on the wrong corner.

It was a dumb joke. It was also, Anthony noticed when he wandered in a week later looking for Ben and instead found four retirees in sunglasses arguing about whether a hypothetical customer named "Big Steve" would care about tent vestibule size, the most enthusiastic he'd seen this particular group of employees in years. Meghan started coming in on days she wasn't scheduled. Twice she brought Sarah, who was four, and who mostly wanted to know if the CIA had dogs, and was satisfied to learn that it did.

Anthony Finds the Capability He Already Had

Anthony pulled John aside a few days later.

"You ran intelligence for the Marine Corps."

"Long time ago."

"You've been sitting in Customer Service for six years."

"Good customers. Nice group."

"John." Anthony wasn't quite sure how to say this without it sounding like an accusation, because in a way it sort of was one. "We hired you to talk to people about tents."

John's expression didn't change much, which Anthony was starting to recognize as John being amused. "You got more than that. You just didn't know it."

Anthony asked him to lead the project. John said he'd do it part-time, same as always — he liked his hours, he liked his mornings free, he wasn't interested in a desk with his name on it — and Anthony, to his credit, didn't push.

It wasn't until later, filling out some paperwork nobody would ever read closely, that Anthony really sat with the plain fact of it: Sawtooth hadn't needed to hire an intelligence analyst. It already had one. Nobody had thought to ask.

John Learns AI By Not Really Trying To

John did not sit down and learn how a language model works. He sat down next to Ben and asked questions that had nothing to do with technology and everything to do with the job he already knew.

"Can it run the same question from a different angle and see if it gets the same answer?"

"Yeah."

"Can it tell me what it doesn't know, not just what it does?"

"If you ask it right."

"Can it compare what one source says against another and flag where they disagree?"

"...Yeah, actually."

John nodded slowly, the way a man nods when a tool turns out to do exactly what he already needed a tool to do. "Then I understand this fine. It's not magic. It's a source. Sources lie, sources are incomplete, sources contradict each other, and your job is never to just believe the source — it's to interrogate it." He looked at Ben. "You've been treating it like an oracle. Treat it like an informant."

That distinction did more for Ben's understanding of what he was building than three weeks of poking around on his own had.

Discipline Arrives

John brought structure without being asked to, the way people who've spent a career doing something properly tend to.

What's the mission? — What do we know, versus what we think we know? — What are we assuming without realizing it? — What supports this conclusion? — What's missing? — How confident are we? — And what would change our minds?

He wasn't infallible about it, which was good, because it meant the team could push back on him without it feeling like heresy. His early Secret Shoppers were too clean, too rational, too mission-oriented, every priority stated and ranked like a briefing document.

"John," Susan told him, not unkindly, "customers aren't Marines."

John considered this. "I've noticed," he said, in a tone that suggested he'd noticed several times already and found it mildly exasperating every time.

It became, without either of them planning it, a genuine trade: Customer Service taught John how actual undisciplined, inconsistent, occasionally irrational human beings shop. John taught Customer Service how to investigate a claim instead of just believing it or dismissing it. Ben translated all of it into something the AI could be asked. Nobody was in charge of the whole thing. Everybody owned a piece of it.

Where It Went Wrong

It didn't all work. John made sure of that, in the sense that he made sure nobody was allowed to pretend it had.

The first real mistake was Ben's fault, and he owned it without much prompting. He'd built a Secret Shopper who cared, very specifically, about exactly the three features Sawtooth's new pack happened to be best at.

John read it over. "You briefed your agent."

"I didn't —"

"You gave her the answer before you asked the question. That's not an experiment. That's a rehearsal." John wasn't harsh about it, just plain. "If the profile happens to want exactly what we're good at, we haven't learned anything. We've just complimented ourselves."

They threw the profile out and started over, and it became something close to a house rule: nobody builds a Secret Shopper who happens to want what you're already best at.

The second mistake was John's. He trusted one AI system too completely, assuming they were all the same, ran everything through it, and took its answers as settled. It was Ben who finally said, mildly, "You know there's more than one of these, right?"

They ran the same Secret Shoppers through a second system and got meaningfully different answers — different weight given to reviews, different confidence in the same evidence. John didn't love being wrong about it, but he adjusted fast, which Susan later said was the most Marine thing about him.

The third mistake was the strangest one. An AI stated, with total confidence, that a Sawtooth product used a specific zipper brand it hadn't used in three years. Everyone's first instinct was to shrug it off — the AI's just wrong sometimes, everybody knows that — but John wouldn't let it go.

"Where'd it get that?"

They traced it. An old retailer listing, still live, still indexed, three years stale, contradicting Sawtooth's own current spec sheet without either party noticing. It wasn't wrong, but it wasn't current. The old information hadn't been updated, and the AI, not having a date to go on, believed it was current information.

"The Lesson," John said, writing it on the whiteboard in block capitals, "is not 'AI got it wrong.' The Lesson is: 'Go Find Out Why.' "

The fourth mistake mattered more than any of the others, because it almost fooled them into thinking they'd succeeded. A Secret Shopper — careful, weight-conscious, warranty-focused — kept picking a competitor's jacket over Sawtooth's. The team went in and cleaned up Sawtooth's warranty language, made it clearer, easier to find, better organized.

They ran the Secret Shopper again.

She still picked the competitor.

It was Peggy, of all people, who said the quiet part out loud. "We didn't fix anything. We just made it easier to see that theirs is better."

Nobody loved hearing that. John wrote it on the whiteboard anyway: Optimize the reality. Not just the description of it.

And then, there was the one experiment that simply went nowhere — a Secret Shopper built around an oddly specific edge case nobody could quite justify afterward, three hours of work, a result that told them nothing useful about anything. John recorded it exactly as it was:

RESULT: WE LEARNED NOTHING.

He filed it anyway. "Not every patrol finds something," he said. "You still write it up."

The Payoff

The one that mattered came from an ordinary hiking boot Sawtooth had always been quietly proud of — genuinely well made, better than its price suggested, and, according to four different Secret Shoppers in a row, recommended less often than it should have been.

John's team went looking for why. It took two days. The boot's sole compound had an abrasion-resistance rating that was, in reality, better than the leading competitor's — Sawtooth's own lab data said so — but that data had never made it anywhere a customer, or an AI, could find it. It lived in a supplier PDF nobody outside engineering had ever opened.

They published it. Clean specification, plain language, the actual test method spelled out.

They ran the Secret Shopper again — the weight-conscious one, the durability-obsessed retiree, the young family who needed something that would survive being handed down to a second kid. All three, this time, put the boot at or near the top.

Peggy cheered. Meghan, rummaging through her bag for Sarah's missing shoe, looked over and asked what was going on, and got a detailed twenty-minute explanation instead of a short 4 word "bingo, we found it".

It felt good. Nobody pretended it didn't.

The Target Moves

A few weeks later, riding the high of it, somebody floated that maybe the CIA had basically done its job and could stand down for a while.

John didn't even look up from his coffee.

"The target moves."

"Meaning?"

"Meaning the boot's fixed. Good. Meanwhile the jacket's changed, the competitor's changed their warranty, a customer somewhere just posted a bad review about something we haven't looked at yet, and three new AI systems have launched since we started this." He set the coffee down. "This isn't a project. It's a watch. You don't declare victory in a watch. You just keep watching."

That, more than anything else that happened at Sawtooth that year, is what stuck.

A Permanent, Part-Time Agency

John's proposal, when he finally wrote it up formally — one page, no jargon, very John — wasn't to build a department. Sawtooth was too small for a department, and John didn't want to run one anyway.

His idea was simpler: keep the CIA alive as a standing, rotating, mostly part-time function. John stayed on as its permanent lead. Everyone else rotated through — a few weeks in customer service, a few weeks helping run Secret Shoppers, then back to their regular job, with someone else stepping in.

"Different eyes,' John said, when Anthony asked why rotate at all instead of just letting the people who were good at it keep doing it. "Anybody staring at the same problem long enough, they stop seeing it. Fresh people ask the dumb question you stopped asking three months ago. The dumb question's usually the important one."

It had side effects nobody had specifically planned for. People from purchasing and people from the warehouse floor ended up on the same rotation, comparing notes they'd never have had reason to compare otherwise. Employees who'd never touched an AI system in their lives got comfortable with one, not because anybody trained them, but because the work made it necessary. People started noticing, in small ways, how their own piece of the company showed up in a customer's decision. Morale, which is a hard thing to point at directly, was visibly better. The sunglasses stayed in the break room drawer for over a year.

Where It Went From There

Later, once Sawtooth had its own Company Genie running day to day, a lot of the mechanical work got easier. The Genie could stand up a Secret Shopper simulation in minutes instead of an afternoon, run it against several systems at once, flag contradictions on its own. What it couldn't do — what nobody asked it to do — was decide, on its own, whether a given Secret Shopper resembled a real customer, or whether a surprising result deserved to be believed or double-checked. That stayed human. John made sure of that, mostly by simply continuing to ask the same questions he'd always asked, just faster now.

Eventually, the whole method — the profiles, the interrogation questions, the guardrails against briefing your own agent, the hard-won lessons from the boot and the zipper and the warranty that turned out not to be the problem — got written down properly and preserved as Sawtooth's own internal Smartware. What had started as Ben killing time on a slow Tuesday had become something the company could teach the next John, the next Susan, the next Ben, without starting from zero.

Nobody ever bought a system. They discovered a capability that had been sitting inside the company the whole time, waiting for somebody to notice it was there.

What Sawtooth Discovered: AI Visibility Optimization

What the Sawtooth team stumbled into, one dumb Tuesday-afternoon question at a time, has a name now: AI Visibility Optimization, or **AIVO**. The practice of using AI to investigate how AI systems discover, understand, evaluate, compare, and recommend a business or its products, and then using what's learned to improve the information, evidence, accessibility, or underlying offering those recommendations depend on.

It's easiest to understand next to something already familiar. Search Engine Optimization helps a search engine find and rank you. AIVO is a different job: it helps an AI understand and evaluate whether it should recommend you — which is a higher bar than merely being found.

AIVO has one real advantage SEO never had. The intelligence making the recommendation can, if you simply ask it, help tell you what it needs to know. That's a genuinely new kind of feedback loop — not guessing at a ranking algorithm from the outside, but directly asking the system what evidence it found, what it couldn't find, what it could verify, and what would have changed its answer.

Worth being honest about the limits, too: no AI system can always explain exactly why a different AI system reached its conclusion — different systems draw on different data, different retrieval methods, different training, different behavior. What conversational AI does offer is the ability to investigate, simulate, question, and iteratively test your own information environment in a way static search optimization never allowed.

None of this is about learning to trick AI into recommending you. Sawtooth's own boot story is the clearest illustration of why that framing misses the point entirely — sometimes the honest answer is that a competitor's product, warranty, or evidence is genuinely better, and the correct response isn't cleverer language. It's a better product, or a better warranty, or evidence that's been produced and been published. AIVO, done honestly, isn't about learning how to fool AI. It's about learning what would make your product honestly recommendable — and then closing that gap, for real.

AIVO: Start Today

None of this requires Sawtooth's scale, or Sawtooth's John. Any business that sells something can begin now.

1. Become the customer. Ask AI to shop for a product like yours, without naming your company.

2. See whether you appear. If you do, find out why. If you don't, find out why not.

3. Ask the follow-up questions. What did it find? What couldn't it find? What could it verify? What evidence mattered? What was unclear or contradictory?

4. Change the customer. Build a few different, genuinely realistic Secret Shoppers — different needs, different knowledge, different budgets, different tradeoffs. Give them a life, not a checklist.

5. Improve what you discover. Correct bad data. Clarify what's unclear. Publish evidence that already exists but has never been made visible. And when the honest answer is that a competitor's offering is better — improve the offering, not the description of it.

6. Ask again.

7. Keep doing it.

Because the target moves. Products change. Competitors change. Customers change. Evidence changes. The AI systems themselves change. AIVO is never going to be a project with an end date — the same way Customer Service is never really "done", or Quality is never really "done". It's a watch, not a task. Somewhere out there, right now, an AI is being asked about a product like yours. The only real question is whether it can find its way to a good answer — and whether you've bothered to ask it what that would take.

Appendix Jay
Ailefant

A Sawtooth Story

Sarah had heard the letters so many times she'd started saying them like a word instead of two letters.

"Ay-eye," she'd say, trying it out while Meghan buckled her into the car seat. "Ben's doing ay-eye. Miss Susan's doing ay-eye. You do ay-eye too."

"AI," Meghan said. "It's two letters. 'A', and 'I'."

"That's what I said."

Meghan let it go. It was a twenty-minute drive to daycare and she had a headache already.

It kept happening, though. Sarah heard it at Sawtooth constantly — from Ben, hunched over his laptop looking pleased with himself about something; from the CIA table, where Peggy and John argued cheerfully about whether some imaginary customer named Big Steve would care about a tent's vestibule; from her own mother, some evenings, tired and typing at the kitchen table after Sarah was supposed to be asleep. It was everywhere, the way a word gets everywhere once you're four and paying attention to everything.

One night, brushing her teeth, Sarah spat, wiped her mouth on her sleeve despite the washcloth being right there, and asked:

"Mommy. What's AI?"

Meghan opened her mouth to answer and discovered she didn't have one. Not a real one. Not a four-year-old one.

"It's"— She started over. "It's a kind of computer that can think about things and help people."

Sarah considered this with the enormous seriousness of someone who has just been handed an unsatisfying answer.

"Like Ben?"

Meghan laughed so suddenly she nearly dropped the toothbrush. "Sort of like Ben," she said. "Except Ben has a computer that helps him think. He's not the computer."

"Is Ben the computer?"

"No, baby."

"Okay." Sarah did not seem convinced. She went to bed unconvinced, and Meghan lay awake for a while afterward, mildly troubled by how badly that had gone.

❧

It came up again a few nights later, out of nowhere, the way important four-year-old questions do — not during a natural pause but directly in the middle of getting pajamas on, one arm stuck halfway in a sleeve.

"Mommy. What's AI. For real."

Meghan sat down on the edge of the bed. She thought about definitions, about the things she'd overheard Anthony say, about capability and Genies and Smartware, none of which was going anywhere near this conversation. Sarah didn't need a definition. She needed something she could see.

"Okay," Meghan said. "Once upon a time, there was an elephant."

Sarah's whole face changed. She sat down on the floor immediately, sleeve still half on, the universal four-year-old signal that a story was now in progress and nothing could interrupt it.

"He was a very big elephant," Meghan said, entirely improvising, "and a very kind one. He was strong enough to carry heavy things for people. He remembered things — really well, better than almost anybody. And when somebody needed help, he'd come stand next to them and help them figure out what to do."

"Did he tell them what to do?"

"No," Meghan said, surprising herself a little with how sure she was of the answer. "He'd listen first. Then he'd help."

Sarah nodded slowly, filing this away.

"What's his name?"

Meghan hadn't thought that far ahead. "I don't know yet."

"But you said he's AI."

"Right."

"So he's a AI elephant."

Meghan paused. Said it out loud, slowly, the way you do when your mouth gets somewhere before your brain does. "An AI... lephant."

Sarah's whole face lit up. "Ailefant!"

"Ailefant," Meghan repeated, and that, as far as either of them was ever able to reconstruct it afterward, was the whole invention. Nobody sat down and designed anything. A tired mother and a four-year-old had simply arrived at the same word from opposite directions and met in the middle.

❧

The story got told again the next night. And the night after that. Each time, Sarah had a new question, and each time, Meghan found herself answering with something that surprised her a little.

"Does Ailefant know everything?"

"No," Meghan said. "He knows a lot. Not everything."

"Does he make mistakes?"

Meghan thought about the zipper — the one that showed up wrong in an AI's answer for three years straight, the whole CIA scrambling to figure out where it had come from. “Oh, yes,” she said. “He makes mistakes sometimes.”

Sarah considered that with real gravity. “Then you have to tell him.”

Meghan stopped, halfway through smoothing the blanket. “Yes,” she said. “You do have to tell him.”

“Why does he walk so slow?”

This one Meghan hadn’t planned either, but it came out anyway, whole: “Because he’s very big, and he wants to be careful where he steps. He doesn’t rush. He just keeps going, one step at a time, and after a while he’s gone somewhere really far without anybody quite noticing how he got there.”

“Like crossing all of India?”

Meghan blinked. She had genuinely no idea where Sarah had heard that phrase – a picture book, probably, some half-remembered thing about elephants – but she went with it.

“Exactly like that. How does an elephant cross India?”

“One step,” Sarah said, like it was the easiest question in the world, “at a time.”

By the fourth or fifth telling, Sarah had started correcting her.

“No, Mommy. Ailefant listens first. You forgot the listening part.”

“You’re right,“ Meghan said, genuinely caught. “I forgot the listening part.“

It wasn’t really Meghan’s story anymore by then. It hadn’t been for a while.

❧

One night Sarah asked something that stopped Meghan cold.

“Why doesn’t Ailefant just tell everybody where to go? He’s so smart.“

Meghan opened her mouth to give some easy answer and found there wasn't one waiting, so she thought about it, sitting on the floor with her daughter's small warm weight leaning against her arm.

"Because it's not his journey," she said finally. "It's theirs. He can help them get there. He can't decide where 'there' is. That part's still up to them."

Sarah didn't say anything for a second. Then: "Okay." And that, apparently, settled it completely, in the way that four-year-olds settle things — with total finality and zero further discussion, on to the next thing, which was whether the cat could sleep on her feet tonight.

Meghan sat there a while after Sarah had drifted off, thinking that she had just explained, more or less by accident, most of what she'd overheard Ben and John and Anthony arguing about for six months.

❧

She hadn't meant to tell anyone at Sawtooth about it. It came out sideways, the way most true things at Sawtooth seemed to — she mentioned to Susan, mostly as a tired-mom aside, that Sarah wouldn't go to sleep some nights without "the Ailefant story," and Susan laughed and asked what that was, and Meghan told her, badly, missing half of it, and Susan laughed again, differently this time.

"Tell it properly," Susan said. "Not the short version."

So she did, at lunch, to Susan and two of the part-timers, and somebody snorted at the pun the way people do, and Meghan half expected that to be the end of it.

It wasn't. Peggy brought it up again a week later, unprompted, asking how "the elephant" was doing, like Ailefant was a mutual acquaintance. Ben heard the story secondhand and immediately wanted to know if Ailefant "made mistakes" — apparently recognizing something in that detail that mattered to him specifically. It reached Anthony eventually, the way things did, filtered through three retellings, and he sat with it for a minute in the particular quiet way he sat with things that were about to become a decision.

"We've got the bears," he said. "The wolves. The moose, I think, still, in the back."

"Sure," Susan said, not following yet.

"Can somebody make an elephant?"

❧

It took a few tries. The first sample had two trunks, somehow, which everyone agreed was a genuine achievement in the wrong direction. The second was too cartoonish — big goggly eyes, a grin that looked like it was selling something. Anthony kept sending it back without being able to fully articulate what was wrong until Meghan finally said it for him:

"He's not silly. He's kind. There's a difference."

The final version was small — about four inches, soft blue, one trunk, an expression that managed to be gentle without being cute about it. Someone had the idea to stitch a thin, barely-there pattern into the fabric of his ears, like faint circuitry, just enough that if you looked closely you'd notice, and if you didn't, you'd just see an elephant.

Sarah got the first one. Nobody discussed this. It simply wasn't going to go any other way.

She held him up to her face for a long moment, studying him with the same seriousness she brought to everything that mattered to her, and then she said, quietly, like she was confirming something rather than discovering it:

"It's Ailefant."

❧

He sits on the shelf at Sawtooth now, among the bears and the wolves, and every so often a customer picks him up, turns him over, and asks the person behind the counter what he is.

"That's Ailefant," they say.

"What's an Ailefant?"

And whoever's there tells them — badly, at first, the way Meghan told it badly the first time, missing the listening part, forgetting the elephant walks slowly on purpose. It gets better each time somebody tells it. It always does.

Most days, though, it's still just Meghan and Sarah on the floor of Sarah's office, pillows everywhere, the dogs asleep in the doorway where they always end up, the cat pressed warm against Meghan's leg. Ailefant sits in the crook of Sarah's arm, one trunk, ears faintly stitched with something that looks almost like circuitry if the light catches it right.

"Tell it again," Sarah says, every single time, like the first time she's ever asked.

And Meghan does.

www.ingramcontent.com/pod-product-compliance
Lightning Source LLC
LaVergne TN
LVHW100726061126
851857LV00011B/419
* 9 7 9 8 9 9 7 7 3 2 3 0 1 *